How to Use Patient Satisfaction Data to Improve Healthcare Quality

Also Available from ASQ Quality Press

Customer Driven Healthcare: QFD for Process Improvement and Cost Reduction
Ed Chaplin, M.D. and John Terninko, Ph.D.

How to Use Control Charts in HealthCare
D. Lynn Kelley

Insights to Performance Excellence in Healthcare 2000:
An Inside Look at the 2000 Baldrige Award Criteria for Healtcare
Mark L. Blazey, Paul Grizzell, Linda Janczak

The Handbook for Managing Change in Health Care
ASQ Health Care Series, Chip Caldwell, editor

Mentoring Strategic Change in Health Care: An Action Guide
Chip Caldwell

Healthcare Performance Measurement: Systems Design and Evaluation
Vahé A. Kazandjian and Terry R. Lied

Stop Managing Costs: Designing Healthcare Organizations Around Core Business Systems
James P. Mozena, Charles E. Emerick, and Steven C. Black

Measuring Customer Satisfaction: Survey Design, Use, and Statistical Analysis Methods
Bob E. Hayes

Customer Satisfaction Measurement and Management
Earl Naumann and Kathleen Giel

Statistical Quality Control Using EXCEL (with software)
Steven M. Zimmerman, Ph.D. and Marjorie L. Icenogle, Ph.D.

To request a complimentary catalog of ASQ Quality Press publications, call 800-248-1946, or visit our online bookstore at qualitypress.asq.org.

How to Use Patient Satisfaction Data to Improve Healthcare Quality

by
Ralph Bell
Michael J. Krivich

ASQ Quality Press
Milwaukee, Wisconsin

Library of Congress Cataloging-in-Publication Data

Bell, Ralph, 1948-

How to use patient satisfaction data to improve healthcare quality / Ralph Bell, Michael J. Krivich.

p. cm.

Includes bibliographical references and index.

ISBN 0-87389-474-X

1. Patient satisfaction. 2. Medical care--Quality control. 3 Medical care surveys. 4. Outcome assessment (Medical care) I. Krivich, Michael J., 1953-II. Title.

RA399.A1 B44 2000

362.1'068'5--dc21

99-058337

10 9 8 7 6 5 4 3 2 1

ISBN 0-87389-474-X

Acquisitions Editor: Ken Zielske
Project Editor: Annemieke Koudstaal
Production Administrator: Shawn Dohogne
Special Marketing Representative: David Luth

ASQ Mission: The American Society for Quality advances individual and organizational performance excellence worldwide by providing opportunities for learning, quality improvement, and knowledge exchange.

Attention: Bookstores, Wholesalers, Schools and Corporations:
ASQ Quality Press books, videotapes, audiotapes, and software are available at quantity discounts with bulk purchases for business, educational, or instructional use. For information, please contact ASQ Quality Press at 800-248-1946, or write to ASQ Quality Press, P.O. Box 3005, Milwaukee, WI 53201-3005.

To place orders or to request a free copy of the ASQ Quality Press Publications Catalog, including ASQ membership information, call 800-248-1946. Visit our web site at www.asq.org. or qualitypress.asq.org.

Printed in the United States of America

 Printed on acid-free paper

American Society for Quality

Quality Press
611 East Wisconsin Avenue
Milwaukee, Wisconsin 53202
Call toll free 800-248-1946
www.asq.org
qualitypress.asq.org
standardsgroup.asq.org

Table of Contents

Preface

The traditional use of patient-satisfaction data has been to show the board of directors, medical staff, employees, and the general community what they already believed, that they provide high-quality patient care. Serious efforts to understand how to analyze patient satisfaction and how to use that information to reduce costs and improve quality are relatively rare. *Feeling good* about your hospital or health system was considered the path to making the institution *good*. Given this definition, it is no wonder that patient satisfaction was never seriously considered as a method to improve quality and reduce costs by listening to what the customer has to say about the quality of services delivered.

With pressures from market-based competition, managed-care organizations, employers, and the government to reduce costs and improve quality, new and innovative ways need to be found to meet these demands. With this in mind, patient satisfaction remains one of the great untapped areas of potential that could help enhance the work of total quality management and continuous quality improvement (TQM/CQI) programs, organizational reengineering, and patient-focused care. As revenues become scarcer and competition more acute, properly analyzed patient-satisfaction data can provide opportunities for service improvement, improved revenue streams, and a superior market position. If healthcare organizations owe patients anything, it is to listen most attentively to their concerns and questions. Patient surveys represent a way patients can voice their concerns about their healthcare. Within this body of information on how the public views our care apparatus lies opportunity, which until now has been largely ignored by the industry.

Our reasons for writing this book stem from our reasonably long experience with healthcare organizations and how they behave. Through our interactions with healthcare administrators, ancillary staff, students in the field, and professional associations, one thing has become clear. Healthcare workers and patients tend to view how the delivery system works very differently. That is, the view of how services are delivered by those in the field can be summarized by one word, *fragmentation*. Everyone talks about the delivery system. The term *system* implies a group of component parts working together as a whole. In contrast, however, many see their roles in the delivery of care as being independent or isolated from the whole. When a critical mass of organizational units view themselves in this manner, fragmentation of service delivery occurs.

No single component of a hospital is truly autonomous or isolated. Systems theory dictates that diminished quality in one area has potentially dramatic implications for other areas of the facility. Patients who become dissatisfied with one aspect of their care are likely to carry that view across their entire stay or visit. Furthermore, patient satisfaction is considered by patients, providers, and payers to be a legitimate measure of the quality of healthcare provided.[1] The implication, of course, is that low satisfaction levels for one or two aspects of care may result in significantly lower subjective assessments of the quality of the entire institution.

Administrators have begun to recognize that changes made in one area of the organization impact on other areas. For example, if the scheduling process for Orthopedics fails, patient referrals to Radiology may become erratic with several simultaneous routings. Such a failure would likely result in extended waiting times in Radiology. Add Emergency Room referrals (with higher priority), and the problem is exacerbated. The waiting line and the waiting time at Radiology become longer. After receiving service at Radiology, the patient must return to Orthopedics only to wait to see the physician once again. The end result is an increased level of dissatisfaction with the total visit. Orthopedics is not an isolated department, nor is Radiology, nor is the ER. What happens in one department affects what happens in others, because they are interdependent parts of the hospital. Patients appear to understand this better than administrators, because that is the way they live and move through the encounter. Administrators, on the other hand, often miss the interdependence of departments, because they tend to treat departments in a fragmented way. That is, each department has a separate budget, its own location on the organization chart, and so on.

Interdependence works the other way as well. If improvements are made in one area, there will be a *spillover* effect to other areas. In other words, if patient-satisfaction scores can be improved, even in a single area, the organization can improve its overall performance and its financial *bottom line*. Improving the patients' view of the institution means that return visits are more likely, the willingness to use other services offered by the organization increases, the status of the facility in the community is elevated, quality improves, and, in general, organizational performance is enhanced.

Our goal is to emphasize that improving the level of patient satisfaction is everyone's business. Elevated patient-satisfaction scores mean improved organizational performance,[2] improved quality,[3] and improved financial performance.[4] We want everyone to take a serious look at their patient-satisfaction data and use what they find to improve. Everyone collects patient-satisfaction data, but not everyone knows what to do with them. We have attempted to provide a strategy for applying the data to obtain meaningful and lasting results.

Chapter 1 introduces the concept of satisfaction as a value-added component of care and shows why patient perceptions of satisfaction are important within the context of the managed-care environment. Also, we examine what determines a culture of satisfaction and why that is important in healthcare.

Chapter 2 is a detailed analysis of the process of satisfaction. Given the body of research and literature available, the authors review the important intervening variables in the process of satisfaction. That is, how do the various components of care interact to produce the satisfied patient? From this discussion, the importance of before, after, and ongoing measurements are discussed. The financial implications of the effects of patient satisfaction on revenue are also discussed with a new model of profitability.

Chapter 3 is the audit guide. Many patient-satisfaction surveys are conducted without thought given to the actual program. One may use a patient-satisfaction vendor, or the program may be entirely an in-house creation. What is important is having the information to understand everything about your patient-satisfaction program so that it can be the best possible program for your institution. Are the surveys valid and reliable? Is this program accomplishing all that it originally set out to do, or did it become just another regulatory requirement and a process that provides no useful information? The audit guide is a complete checklist designed to assist in the process of determining the effectiveness of your patient-satisfaction program. Additionally, the pros and cons of different patient-satisfaction methods are discussed. We view patient satisfaction as an optimal component of the quality improvement process rather than as an isolated measurement strategy.

Chapter 4 is the *nuts-and-bolts* section of the text. This chapter illustrates how to effectively analyze patient satisfaction using statistical-process-control tools. This is a practical explanation of what the *voice of the customer* is and what patient-satisfaction data are telling you about the process of care in your institution. This is not just a theoretical discussion but a practical guide to applying the tools to the data and examples of how to set up the systems.

The focus of Chapter 5 is contained in its title, "Applying Interventions for Quality Improvement." In order to make effective use of patient-satisfaction data, the organization must make a long-term commitment to the process. This includes providing ongoing measurement, creating a culture of satisfaction, and determining the financial impact of the satisfaction program. These topics are discussed as they relate to using patient-satisfaction data.

Chapter 6 is a case study of a fictitious hospital using the techniques presented in earlier chapters to make a meaningful positive impact in improving one aspect of patient satisfaction. The statistical-process-control tools are applied to a particular scenario and discussed with the appropriate graphs and tables provided. The focal issue in the case study is nurse-patient communication and what was done to improve patient perceptions.

Chapter 7 concludes the text with a summary of all of the previous discussion. Some general guidelines of what tools to use and when are provided.

Examples, charts, tables, and diagrams are provided throughout the text to reinforce the concepts presented. This book is intended for those involved in patient satisfaction, quality, and risk management; marketing; and market research. It is also intended for graduate students in health-administration programs to augment their understanding of and application of the tools of quality. Most importantly, it is intended for those senior healthcare leaders that heretofore have viewed patient satisfaction as just another required outcome measure rather than as a valuable tool to be used to enhance organizational performance.

Finally, we would like to say a word about the *hospital focus* of this book. We tend to focus on the hospital as the unit of analysis for several reasons. First, the hospital is still at the forefront of medical care in the United States and remains a major focal point for patient concerns. Second, hospitals have been formally involved in the patient-satisfaction data collection process longer than other entities. Third, although patient satisfaction is of considerable importance for managed-care organizations (MCOs), integrated delivery systems (IDSs), and other healthcare delivery arrangements, the procedure we discuss in this book can be universally applied. Hospitals tend to have the greatest current investment in measuring patient satisfaction and are surely the most complex organizational structures in which the data can be integrated into an organization-wide CQI strategy. The application of our approach to smaller entities (e.g., physician group practices) is straightforward. Similarly, extending the procedures to an IDS simply requires aggregation of data across the system. The successful implementation of these procedures across a system involves applying what works in one area and spreading the success across other areas.

Ralph Bell
Michael J. Krivich

ACKNOWLEDGMENTS

In the course of writing this book, we have included some of our previous work. This work is not solely the writings of the two authors. It also represents much current and past research into patient satisfaction; and the many references throughout this text represent our thankfulness to others. In particular, we would like to thank Goal QPC for permission to use the A value tables for the statistical control charts from *The Memory Jogger*[5] and the voice-of-the-customer diagrams from the 1995 research report, *The Voice of the Customer.*[6] Also, we would like to acknowledge Mark Boyd for his work on developing the early versions of the control charts in chapter 4.

We would like to share our sincere appreciation for E-mail technology, which enabled us to complete this book in a timely fashion. Finally, we would like to thank our families for their encouragement and support in writing this text.

Ralph Bell
Michael J. Krivich

Chapter 1

INTRODUCTION

The difference between data and information is that while data are crudely aggregated collections of raw facts, information represents the selective organization and imaginative interpretation of those facts.
— Theodore Levitt, *The Marketing Imagination*, 1983

THE FOCUS OF THIS BOOK

There are a number of excellent texts focusing on how to collect patient-satisfaction data (see, for example, *Measuring and Managing Patient Satisfaction*).[7] This book is not about how to collect patient-satisfaction data; it is about how to take data and turn them into useful information. It is not about how to design patient surveys; it is about how to use survey data by organizing them in a way to change the processes of care. This book is not about construct validity and reliability of surveys; it is about the voice of the customer informing healthcare administrators what works and what does not work. This book is about a willingness to apply the concepts of total quality management (TQM) and continuous quality improvement (CQI) to patient satisfaction in a rational, organized manner. If applied properly and taken seriously, the results will be higher-quality care, lower costs, and an improved market position.

A focus on patient satisfaction is a relatively new phenomenon. It was not that long ago that patients seemed to be an unlimited resource for healthcare providers. If patients became dissatisfied with their healthcare and chose to switch their source of care, healthcare facilities firmly believed there were "plenty

1

more where they came from." Patient satisfaction therefore was of neither practical nor theoretical interest. In the seventies and eighties, however, patient satisfaction did become a phenomenon of theoretical interest to health-services researchers. For example, patient satisfaction became useful as an indicator of a subjective measure of realized access to care.[8] As such, satisfaction with care became a dependent variable of research interest, as well as a predictor of healthcare outcomes, including compliance with medical advice and return visits for care.[9,10]

Today, we face an unprecedented revolution in healthcare. The informed consumer—through an information explosion propelled by scientific and technological advances, mass media coverage, and the Internet—better understands treatment options and is not afraid to challenge healthcare providers if the care does not meet his or her standards. Since patients can no longer be viewed as an unlimited resource, the consumers have taken control and, in some cases, have more information regarding their specific diagnoses than their healthcare providers. Information flow helps set the standards for individual health behavior and for patient involvement in the diagnostic, treatment, and curative processes.

PATIENT SATISFACTION IS VALUE ADDED

Ease of access to health-related information has spawned a change in the basic healthcare value equation. Traditionally, healthcare value is seen as being a function of cost and quality:

$$V = f \text{ (cost, quality)}$$

As market differentiation decreases in importance, cost and quality become perceived as being equal. In this market situation, value in healthcare is defined as

$$V = f \text{ (cost, quality, satisfaction)}$$

where value is now a function of cost, quality, and satisfaction.

With cost and quality being equal across providers, satisfaction becomes the determining variable when a choice is to be made among providers. In other words, patient satisfaction is *value added*. In this case, utilization and health plan reenrollment decisions, when costs are equal, will be based on patient perceptions of quality and satisfaction with a provider. As healthcare moves toward a more market-driven competitive model and quality equalizes, satisfaction continues to assume increasing importance. Services such as cardiology, oncology, obstetrics, pediatrics, emergency room, and radiology, to name a few, are in abundant supply. Physicians and patients have ample opportunity to "sample" providers. Therefore, in a market where all providers look essentially the same, satisfaction becomes a major competitive tool in attracting customers. Employers and insurance companies increasingly view patient-satisfaction data as one of the measures differentiating providers from one another.[7] Satisfaction levels below benchmark standards have the potential to force health plans to discontinue contracts with providers. Satisfaction levels higher than the benchmark standards can provide an organization with arguments necessary to encourage certain managed-care plans to enter into new contractual arrangements.

There is no doubt that cost and quality move together. Yet, process-redesign strategies in healthcare typically ignore patient satisfaction. To date, these strategies have been clinically or operationally data driven, focusing on what is internal to the hospital. It would make sense, then, that as these internal strategies are exhausted, the attention and focus of quality improvement efforts should shift to patient satisfaction. With 10 years of reengineering process efforts in place, the question becomes *How long can the consultants continue to sell a 26 percent to 40 percent reduction in operating expense?* At some point, attention must turn to the voice of the customer. We believe patient-satisfaction data give us valuable information about the process of care in our institutions. Properly analyzed, patient-satisfaction data can point to areas of patient concern, which when corrected will improve quality, reduce costs, and bring the patient back into the process of care.

Positive patient-satisfaction data generally bring smiles and good feelings to members of a healthcare organization. Typically, satisfaction scores are good to excellent, with ratings for many providers commonly scoring in the 90th percentile. Peer group comparisons fall in the same area. So, why change something that is good and desirable? Think for a minute about the incongruity we face when we see newspaper articles or press reports indicating that consumers rank healthcare providers somewhere slightly above the airline industry in areas of consumer relations and satisfaction. This paints a very different picture from what our surveys show us. We often come to believe that it is a problem for the *other guys*, not us. We paint a glowing picture for the board of directors and medical executive committee that we are doing all the right things. We provide them with aggregate data scores alluding to a flat, linear trend line, neither moving up nor down but essentially remaining static over time.

How do you use patient satisfaction to improve the quality of healthcare? That is the focus of this book. It is not about regression formulas, tight statistical sampling, or even the construct validity or reliability of the survey instrument that you use, although these things are important. As we have noted, there are several other excellent how-to books available to assist in these areas. This book is about how to use a commonsense CQI approach to patient satisfaction and how to recognize what patient-satisfaction data are telling you about the process of care in your institution. Perhaps most important among these is how your patients perceive the quality of the care you provide.

HOW PATIENTS CHOOSE HOSPITALS

There was a time in the not-so-distant past when patients chose hospitals based on the direction of their personal physician. As long as the physician believed that the hospital provided quality care, the patient used that professional judgment as a proxy for their own decision making. Society played an important role as well. Growing up, individuals were taught that the physician has the training, knowledge, and experience to make proper and accurate medical decisions. The general public could not make treatment decisions and did not have access to information to make informed choices. Therefore, the physician was the decision maker in a somewhat parental role, and the patient assumed the role of child in the relationship.[11] Without information, the patient was unable to make medical decisions and could not speak intelligently regarding potential courses of action or outcomes. The skill and the power of the physician were beyond question to the average person.

Enter the age of *deductibles, managed care, patient responsibility,* and a seemingly endless amount of *information.* These four things have done more to change the landscape of personal involvement in healthcare than anything else. The two most important of these may be managed care and information.

Spiraling healthcare costs drove employers to seek ways to reduce their overall healthcare expenditures as a percentage of their overall cost structure. The reasons are well documented. The end results of the movement to reduce operating costs were to *off-load* and shift some of the responsibility to the consumer. Shouldering more of the responsibility for payment required consumers to obtain more information, better understand services offered, and make better choices among competing providers. Once the consumer had an active role in the decision-making process, the dynamics changed on how providers were selected. That is, traditionally, patients chose their physician first and used the hospital where the physician had privileges. Now, patients often select a hospital first based on where their managed-care plan has contracted, then follow by selecting a physician from the available pool. This is not to understate the influence of the physician, which remains strong today, but the dynamics have changed with respect to individual responsibility. Evidence suggests that patient assessments of the quality of care provided by a hospital are related to how they rate physician care.[4,12]

So, for many reasons it is necessary to understand how patients choose hospitals and what the role of patient satisfaction might be. Over the past 20 years, significant research has been conducted regarding this topic. Lane and Lindquist[13] reviewed 15 studies searching for the common thread. Not surprisingly, *quality* is mentioned time and again and is in the top five places overall. The consumer/patient describes quality as personal treatment, the availability of nurses when needed, friendly and courteous staff (both medical and administrative), a willingness to listen, an understandable explanation of treatment, the availability of latest technology and equipment, the availability of specialists with a regional or national reputation, and comfort and appearance of the patient's room.

Next on this list is what the patients describe as *access to care.* Consumers are very aware of what resources are available in the community to meet their emergent and nonemergent healthcare needs. Location of the facility in relation to employment has assumed new importance, as have such amenities as convenient parking for visitors. Services available on weekends and during evening hours are important as well. In addition, reputation and recommendation of family and friends figure into the access judgments made by patients.

Given what we know about patient judgments that influence the selection of the hospital for care, it is clear that there has been a shift in the dynamics of choice. The patient has become the primary decision maker, and the physician has become a secondary influence. One could expect that this trend would continue to grow stronger as patients become more proactive regarding their healthcare treatment. This represents a significant change from the reactive medicine practiced in the past—before the advent of managed care—to a more proactive stance. Several studies have concluded that patient assessments are a major determining factor in decisions to change providers or healthcare plans.[14,15,16] Patient satisfaction is the key to meeting these market challenges and changing perceptions.

WHY ARE PATIENT PERCEPTIONS OF CARE IMPORTANT?

There are several reasons why all healthcare institutions should be concerned about patient perceptions of quality and their level of satisfaction. First, patients who are satisfied are more compliant.[9,10]

That is, they will follow treatment protocols more completely. Second, satisfied patients are more likely to return for follow-up visits,[14,17] complete drug regimens,[7] and in the process get well faster. Third, patient-satisfaction data provide managers with useful information regarding the outcomes of care. Since satisfaction can be viewed as a proxy measure for the outcome of care, patient perceptions can point out process areas needing improvement.[3,18] Fourth, patient satisfaction is a subjective measure of access to care.[18] A fifth reason is that patients who are satisfied tend to litigate less.[19,20] Sixth, satisfied patients, even if the medical outcome is not positive, tend to view the healthcare they were provided as a quality experience if they were satisfied with the level of care provided.[7] Finally, patients, like all consumers, deserve to be satisfied with the product that they purchase.[21]

As hospitals and health systems develop a continuum of care, levels of satisfaction with service across the continuum assume critical importance. Although the hospital may drive health plan decision making, it is no longer the focal entry point into a healthcare system. Take the scenario where an individual may be given an order for a magnetic resonance imaging (MRI) by his or her physician. Depending on the managed-care plan in which the individual is enrolled and co-payment established, this person has several options. One option is that the patient could obtain the needed service at the hospital. Choosing this option will be determined by a number of factors. One consideration will be the availability of a convenient appointment time. In other words, *Can I do this now, or must I come back at another time?* Another issue might be the travel distance from the consumer's geographic origin. Perhaps most important, past experience and satisfaction with the process of obtaining needed services from the provider are likely to be major determinants.

In situations where the patient has a variety of choices, the most satisfying previous experience in terms of travel distance, time, cost, trouble-free process, and so on will most determine which option will be selected. All things equal, individuals are likely to make their choice decisions based on levels of satisfaction. In the preceding example, the patient could choose to obtain the

MRI at your diagnostic outpatient facility, in your hospital, or from a freestanding, competitive MRI center. Basically, the patient could choose to experience the service from your facility or from a competing health system. If the option selected is outside your health system, the result is not only lost revenue for the current services but also the very real risk that the patient will move to a different provider permanently, taking future revenues away from your facilities.

Querying patients about all dimensions of the care they receive across the health system provides the opportunity to identify areas where the process of care fails to provide an encompassing, satisfying experience. Satisfaction is a valuable weapon that provides an edge in a highly competitive marketplace. If you are not using available tools to understand and interpret patient-satisfaction data, you are missing valuable opportunities for improvement. Patient-satisfaction data reflect the voice of the customer. That voice provides a very personal view of the process of care within your institution.

Patients typically do not view their healthcare experience as a set of isolated events, but the tendency for hospitals today is to continue to view the process of care through *silos*. Admissions does this; transport did that; the laboratory phlebotomist did that; nursing provided this; and so forth. In the typical hospital inter-disciplinary care meeting, where each person reports on what they did to achieve a coordinated approach to care, patient satisfaction with process is rarely discussed or reported upon. Management still compartmentalizes the organization and believes the patient does the same.

Patients, on the other hand, view the hospital or healthcare experience as a set of interrelated events. *How well did admissions facilitate my entry to the hospital? How well did nursing communicate with the laboratory on the timing of the blood sample drawn? How well did the radiology department interact with food service and internal transportation in scheduling my tests? Did I go for a test at mealtime to come back and find a cold dinner?* The patient's judgments of his or her healthcare experience provide the basic information necessary to make decisions regarding whether or not this was a quality care experience. These judgments determine whether the patient is satisfied or dissatisfied with the experience and ultimately determine whether he or she will return for care in the future. Even within the context of a simpler, routine office visit, the patient's level of satisfaction with the care provided contributes to judgments concerning the quality of that care.

KNOWLEDGE IS POWER

Much of the change experienced by the healthcare system in terms of patient perception of care is due to the consumer information explosion that is sweeping the industry. Ten or fifteen years ago, healthcare information and the knowledge base it supports were limited to practitioners. Limiting access to basic medical information resulted in a greater reliance on the professional in control of that information. Professionals possessed a body of knowledge to which the consumer did not have access. The result was a wide knowledge gap and an asymmetrical relationship between the patient and the provider, with power in the hands of the practitioner.[22] Today, however, consumers have access to more information about diseases and treatments than ever before, reducing the knowledge gap and equalizing the patient-practitioner relationship.[21]

Internet websites, such as *WebMD, American Health Network*, and *Dr. Koop's Health Information*, provide the average consumer with much (if not too much) health-related information. For example, suppose a child develops an unknown rash. Through contacting the physician's office and describing the symptoms, the practitioner informs the parent that the child most likely has Fifth disease. Fifth disease has no treatment because it is a viral infection. The parent, interested in more information, searches the Internet for sites containing medical information. The search results in locating a website with the uniform resource locator (URL) of drkoop.com. Once on this website, the parent can access the *Pediatric Encyclopedia* to find Fifth disease. The disease is described in lay terminology, alternate names, and prevention strategies; and symptoms are described. Even in this one small isolated example, the parent has moved from complete dependence on the provider to becoming an informationally well-armed individual. Yet never once did the practitioner recommend the Internet as a source of information. This represents the proactive consumer–driven medicine of today, not the reactive consumer medicine of the recent past.

In addition, hospitals and health systems, through advertising, quarterly magazines, and direct mail campaigns, provide additional healthcare information upon which consumers make choices. Further, television and radio stations, as well as the print media, regularly provide health, medical, and technology updates as part of their public service efforts. Taken together, the result is a much better educated patient who wants to be an active and willing participant in the healthcare process. Thus, the traditional view of the patient as a docile recipient of medical care must be replaced with the notion that the patient is a knowledgeable consumer of care.[21,23]

With knowledge comes power and the ability to make informed choices and decisions. Traditionally, power within the patient-practitioner relationship was maintained by the physician by limiting the access to medical knowledge required to make the patient healthy.[22,24] Healthcare consumers, however, are no longer passive individuals who are content to *let medical care happen to them.* Easy access to information makes the patient better informed and more involved in decision making regarding treatment options and courses of care. An informed consumer demands a higher level of service excellence and expects to be listened and responded to and treated with dignity and respect. With respect to satisfaction, this means that patients as informed consumers are able to make qualitative decisions about the process of care. Patient perceptions of satisfaction have become extremely valuable to healthcare organizations. Again, the point is that patient-satisfaction data is the voice of the customer and reflects the process of care in your institution. Patient-satisfaction perceptions are well grounded in the facts of their experience. These direct experiences highlight what the informed consumer perceives as good and desirable, as well as what needs improvement.

SATISFACTION AND EMPLOYERS

As hospital and health systems enter into direct contracts with employers, employee satisfaction becomes a critical variable in obtaining and retaining contracts. In a self-insured environment, the employer may look to contract with a single hospital and its medical staff to provide necessary medical care. All things being equal, why should an employer choose your hospital or health system?

One reason may be that you have the geographic coverage to meet the health needs of the employees no matter where they live. Another could be that your price for basic services is better than others. Yet a third reason could be that your reputation for high quality and customer-friendly services places you head and shoulders above the competition. The only way that you would know this is through understanding how that employer's employees feel about the care they receive at your institution. The last thing that an employer needs is complaints from its workers regarding the health service that is less than satisfactory. Understanding the nature of customer service and perceptions, employers expect the same levels of service from their healthcare providers as their customers expect from them. By reporting results back to the employer, customer-satisfaction data provide a powerful way to keep and hold contracts in a highly competitive environment. Yet, if you cannot monitor satisfaction by an employer, you are not negotiating at full strength. If you are not monitoring satisfaction by employers, you risk finding out one day that a direct contract and the revenue associated with it is gone because of dissatisfaction levels that are unacceptable to the employer.

What you are attempting to create with employers is not different from that with your patients and physicians—a loyal customer who would never consider or think of going elsewhere to meet their healthcare needs. Revenue generation in the form of repeat business follows satisfaction.

SATISFACTION AND THE MANAGED-CARE ENVIRONMENT

An interesting phenomenon that is taking shape concerns the reformation of managed care. Specifically, we are witnessing a new freedom to choose physicians and providers within what has been viewed by consumers as a restrictive organizational structure. The consumer-choice backlash appears to work against the fundamental principles of managed care. That is, managed-care organizations have attempted to limit choice, control the medical loss ratio, and offer lower premiums than the competition to gain market share. Using the law of large numbers, combined with the ability to share risk across a spectrum of individuals, managed-care organizations have established deep provider discounts resulting in large operating margins. Employers primarily shop for health insurance on the basis of price. Closed physician panels, limited providers, and deep discounts by hospitals and other health providers offer the basis for control of escalating premiums.

Yet, with the growing patient-as-educated-consumer movement and poor public relations efforts on the part of the managed-care industry, limited choice is beginning to be replaced by point-of-service (POS) plans, open physician panels, and a choice of acute-care providers. In response, the managed-care industry has begun to focus on patient-satisfaction ratings of its physicians and hospital members. By establishing satisfaction benchmarks, decisions to move physicians and hospitals into and out of networks are based on consumer feedback. There is evidence to support the notion that managed-care organizations select physicians and negotiate compensation packages based on patient-satisfaction scores.[25,26,27] As consolidation continues within the managed-care industry, customer retention has become a major focus, if not a major concern. It follows that as differentiation among plans becomes less apparent, customer service and levels of satisfaction become critical decision and control variables. The marketing adage that it costs five times as much to gain a new customer as it costs to retain an existing member comes into play.[28] Therefore, using patient-satisfaction data to improve healthcare quality meets a need being expressed by managed-care organizations. Even in situations where managed-care companies have established exclusive provider relations, employers have the ability to break those relationships by demanding that particular providers be included in their health plans. Healthcare providers have the ability to create that market demand through the effective use of patient satisfaction and by providing customer service that surpasses established benchmarks. Finkelstein and colleagues conclude that patient assessments of the healthcare they receive is useful for differentiating among hospitals.[29] Patient-satisfaction data, when used by patients, providers, employers, and payers, represents key information on which institutions provide high-quality care and on which institutions do not. Customer satisfaction ultimately becomes a controllable, competitive, and strategic tool in high-stakes negotiations with managed-care organizations.

However, this important and controllable factor cannot be utilized if a culture of satisfaction does not exist within the institution. Patient satisfaction is not a program. It is not a slogan, nor is it a platitude hanging on the wall of an institution. It is and must be embraced as a way of life in an organization that seeks first and foremost to create a highly satisfied customer. In a competitive marketplace, such a culture of satisfaction is what stands between a premier marketplace success or being an "also ran." Disney, Nieman Marcus, Home Depot, Johnson and Johnson, Hewlit Packard, 3M, and The Ritz Carlton all stand as examples of successful companies competing and winning based on providing services or products resulting in high levels of customer satisfaction. The satisfied customer returns while the dissatisfied customer finds an alternative place to spend his or her money.

Name one hospital or health system that carries the weight the aforementioned companies carry in regard to customer satisfaction. It is a sad testimonial to a highly personal and complex industry that well-known examples do not exist. Most certainly, there are examples in the industry of hospitals that are chosen in the marketplace based on providing superior customer service. Unfortunately, they remain a mystery in today's healthcare environment.

SATISFACTION, REGULATORY AGENCIES, AND REPORT CARDS

The Joint Commission for Accreditation of HealthCare Organizations (JCAHO), the National Committee for Quality Assurance (NCQA), Health Plan Employer Data and Information Set (HEDIS), ISO 9000, many state agencies, and the Malcolm Baldrige National Quality Award competition all consider patient satisfaction to be of importance.[30] All contain regulations and guidelines for the measurement and reporting of specific satisfaction indicators. Many hospitals, health systems, and business cooperatives are publishing report cards with those same patient-satisfaction indicators in an attempt to differentiate themselves in a crowded market. The intent here is not to go through each indicator but to discuss in broad general terms the implications to you as a hospital or health system executive.

Once you have patient-satisfaction data, what are you going to do with them? Some organizations inform their market about the attributes of a particular product or service and claim high levels of satisfaction for a competitive advantage. That is where the agencies and the institutions that measure patient satisfaction only to be in compliance fall short. Patient-satisfaction data should be more than an exercise. By taking regulatory indicators one step further, analysis and action to improve levels of satisfaction give new meaning to the regulations. This text is designed to give you more useful information and the strategies to adapt to any changes that may come in the future. It seems plausible to us that, at some point in the future, you will be asked, *What are you doing with the satisfaction data you collect?* Your choice is either to be proactive and establish a history of accomplishment by improving quality and reducing cost by listening and responding to the voice of your customer or to be reactive and strain to change your organization overnight to meet new demands. That is, you can collect and report data solely to meet the requirements of these organizations or you can collect and analyze patient-satisfaction data, then act upon them going beyond what is required to achieve certification.

As a competitive weapon and to inform consumers, hospitals and health systems today regularly publish satisfaction indicators. Sometimes compared to benchmarks but often not, the results are heralded as why the general public chose one hospital or system over others. In some cases, advertising is created to reflect that we have better communication skills in an effort to differentiate providers in the marketplace. Many times it is a way to use the data that has been collected for regulatory purposes. These report cards serve to bring to light what is good about a particular institution. It is our belief that in market positioning, a proactive and dynamic patient-satisfaction strategy that is carried out to make significant organizational changes on the quality and cost front is more useful to the public than just reporting how much people like the institution. Holding yourself accountable forces change to enhance the overall performance of the organization. Patient-satisfaction data, correctly used internally and in the external marketplace, are a means to achieve new levels of operational performance and meet the informational needs of your community.

SETTING THE BENCHMARK

What this book is about is assisting you in finding nontraditional ways to improve quality and reduce cost by focusing on what your customer has to say about you. It is about setting the benchmark for a level of performance that others follow. Using a third-party company with a large comparative database to set the standard is an important development in measuring patient satisfaction. It gives you an average score to aim for.

Yet, successful organizational performance is not based upon being average. It is based on a concerted effort to be the best. Setting the standard and becoming the benchmark for others are time after time the hallmark of the high-performing organization. In healthcare, this most often is described as the hospital that has exceptional margins, the lowest cost, or the fewest FTEs per adjusted occupied bed. These measures, however, are simply financial in nature.

In other industries, high-performance organizations are recognized for their exceptional financial performance resulting from customer service and are considered to be the class of their industry. They set the benchmark that others attempt to emulate but fall far short of. In healthcare, this kind of operational performance and measurement to become the class of the industry can be accomplished through the effective use of patient-satisfaction data. Healthcare is far from being able to accomplish this task, because no program exists today for using patient-satisfaction data in their most effective manner.

THE CULTURE OF PATIENT SATISFACTION

What are the characteristics of an organization that has a culture of patient satisfaction? First, the culture of satisfaction is a way of life in the organization. The bottom line is not the central focus; rather, the focus centers on a desire and drive to understand the needs of and please the customer completely. The culture of satisfaction must start at the top of the organization. From the president, through senior management, to the front line and service staff at the bottom of the organizational chart, universally everyone knows what the customer-service standards are, what the customer-service behaviors are, and what the focus of the organization is. Accordingly, high-performance organizations establish profiles containing key service-provision attributes of individuals they seek to hire. A culture of satisfaction includes having a set of supportive policies and procedures in human resources and compensation/incentive programs that reward excellent customer service. Rewards for service excellence are based on bonuses, not on unvalued perquisites such as a special parking place for the employee of the month.

A culture of satisfaction promotes the concept that the bottom line is not the sole focus. Value per share cannot be the organization's sole driving force. Healthcare organizations with a culture of patient satisfaction understand value beyond the immediate service or point of contact they bring to their customer. Of course, this does not mean that successful companies who are customer focused do not pay attention to the bottom line. Quite to the contrary. They have a well-grounded understanding of the financial value of their companies. They understand the need to make a profit to fund shareholder equity, to invest in new capital improvements, and to fund research and development. These companies understand that, ultimately, customers are the source of profits and will return for service because they know and respect the organization and are satisfied with the services they receive. Furthermore, these companies also understand that the customers are free to choose where they obtain goods and services. This is a valuable lesson for healthcare. Patients are free to choose which physicians they utilize, where they go for diagnostic workup, and which hospitals, among many options, they will use.

For all practical purposes, healthcare has become a commodity. Healthcare is bought, sold, and traded without thought of allegiance or loyalty to one provider. In fact, over the past 10 years, the healthcare sector has been the top Wall Street performer, surpassing all other investment sectors. If managed care has taught us anything, it is that physician loyalty to patients is a myth. Because physicians have economic needs, they will reject a contract on the basis of an insufficient fee schedule. If this happens, current patients will be left out in the cold when they find out that their personal physician or hospital does not accept their managed-care plan. If no assistance to find another physician or healthcare provider is offered, the patient may feel abandoned in the process. Why, then, do healthcare providers seem puzzled when patients are not loyal to them? The new bottom line should be a maximized level of patient satisfaction. A central focus on providing patients with unparalleled service, as in other industries, will keep them coming back for care. In turn, the financial bottom line will take care of itself.

An important feature of the culture of satisfaction is that it uses data to drive improvement. It does not use operational data, however; it uses customer-focused data. Customer-focused data alerts the organization to potential problems and provides continuous feedback to the organization. The voice of the customer is the single most important piece of market intelligence available. These data reflect that voice and answer questions concerning what can be done to improve customers' perceptions of the process of care. The culture of satisfaction emphasizes continually measuring and listening to the voice of the customer to improve healthcare quality. In the end, the result will be enhanced market position, improved performance, and financial well-being.

SUMMARY

The importance of maintaining satisfied consumers cannot be overstated. Research has shown that patient satisfaction is related to a number of other patient outcomes. Just as important, however, is the idea that patient satisfaction is integral to ensuring the success of a hospital or healthcare organization. Satisfied patients return for care. Dissatisfied patients find another alternative. Attracting and keeping a solid patient base, in turn, provides needed revenues. Even in the managed-care environment, we are witnessing a renewed interest in patient satisfaction, because it has become recognized as a valuable management tool. Patient-satisfaction data reflect the voice of the customer and provide the clues necessary to improve service delivery. Ultimately, such improvements are reflected in an institution's financial bottom line.

Setting the benchmark, improving operational performance, exceeding the requirements of regulatory and third-party agencies, and winning awards can be accomplished by using patient-satisfaction data to drive and sustain quality improvement. Competitive market differentiation, market positioning, and improved organizational performance are possible through the effective use of patient-satisfaction data.

Chapter 2

THE PROCESS OF SATISFACTION

INTRODUCTION

In chapter 1, we discussed the culture of satisfaction and how the changing healthcare environment is making patient satisfaction an imperative for organizational survival. Throughout chapter 2, we will examine the intervening variables that influence the process of satisfaction from the eyes of the patient. In doing so, a section of this chapter is devoted to the consideration of the importance of before and after measurements. Furthermore, the financial implications of patient satisfaction will be examined because, in today's marketplace, patient satisfaction is a driving force behind financial success, capable of generating millions of dollars in revenue for those who can master its intricacies. It can also result in vast losses for those who cannot adapt.

INTERVENING VARIABLES IN THE PROCESS OF SATISFACTION

The process of creating a satisfied patient is a complicated mixture of a number of variables. It is important to remember that patients view the hospital-care experience from a perspective of totality. That is, whether one is satisfied with a given service or product is determined by the interconnectedness of the various components of that experience. However, despite this view of the experience, some variables are more important than others. Concentration on the most important variables can bring about swifter improvements in satisfaction, quality, outcomes, performance, and financial success.

One key variable in improving patient-satisfaction levels is *communication.* This is not rocket science, but patients expect a high level of communication between the provider of care, related organizational units, and themselves. Individuals in today's healthcare environment expect to be listened to, talked with (not at), and involved in the healthcare decision-making process. What we are talking about is not nominal courtesy, such as a kind smile or a nodding of the head and walking away. We are talking about real patient-provider communication that treats individuals with respect, understanding, and dignity throughout the hospital stay. Paul Lane and Jay Lindquist[13] examined the research evidence gathered during the 1980s on hospital choice by consumers. In their review of those findings, provider-patient communication was consistently ranked as one of the indicators of quality care. A recent study of the relationship between a physician's simple acknowledgement of a breast cancer patient's emotional state significantly reduces the anxiety levels in those patients[31]. In as little as 40 seconds, a physician can communicate a sense of compassion for the patient's condition, which will reduce the patient's anxiety about their disease. Patients who are less anxious about their condition are more likely to understand and recall treatment options outlined by the physician. As a result, patients are better able to make informed decisions about their treatment. Presumably, this should also result in more highly satisfied patients.

Carey and Seibert reinforced the strength of this communication effect their study of a large patient-satisfaction database.[32] They found that nurse communication descriptors such as answering questions satisfactorily, feeling comfortable sharing concerns, and being treated like a person and not a disease are important in patients' judgments of quality for the nursing-care scale. The better the communication between the nurse and the patient, the higher the patient's satisfaction level. A lack of communication could result in lost or misinterpreted information, which leads to negative outcomes.[33] In effect, the more complete the communication about the care process and its effects, the more likely it is that satisfaction scores will increase.

Physician behavior is also an important intervening variable in the process of patient satisfaction. In a 1992 study examining the link between quality and hospital profitability, physicians' technical judgments of a hospital's level of quality were, for the most part, in agreement with patients' experience-based views.[34] This implies that patients actually can be good evaluators of quality even though they may lack technical expertise.[35] How patients view physicians, how they interact within the patient-practitioner relationship, and how physicians and patients communicate with one another influence satisfaction levels. Though it has been demonstrated consistently in the literature that nurse behavior is the primary influence on patient satisfaction with hospital services, the physician is also of major importance. What is important is not to lose sight of physician behavior as a major influence on patient satisfaction. Merry suggests that it is imperative to bring physicians into the improvement process as active and willing participants.[36] He maintains that physicians will accept an organizational improvement strategy if they can be convinced they will be "empowered to:

- gain greater certainty over economic stability,
- maintain sufficient clinical freedom to deal with the uncertainties of patient care,
- gain a greater sense of participation and proactive influence in institutional development in the future, and
- restore a lost sense of social value in physicians' work" (p. 58).

As previously stated, patients can and do make judgments about the technical competency of the hospital. Judgments regarding technical capability, treatment options, and state-of-the-art diagnostic procedures are perceived as indicators of quality care by patients. Even if the patient's perception of technical quality is faulty, his or her views are obviously important factors relating to organizational success. The research conducted by Finkelstein, Harper, and Rosenthal indicates that patient views of hospital quality can be useful in helping consumers make provider choice decisions.[37] Patients' subjective views of the healthcare process form the basis for their decision-making strategies when choices concerning future care are made. A patient who is dissatisfied with the perceived quality of care he or she received is likely to go elsewhere, even if objective indicators of quality are strong. Importantly, Mayer and colleagues have demonstrated that customer-service training programs can improve the ways physicians interact with patients.[38] The end result, of course, is elevated patient-satisfaction levels.

The quality of the medical staff is an intervening variable as well. It is one of the most consistent items that appear in research studies of consumer purchase behavior. The combination of a perceived high-quality medical staff and the availability of specialists to meet the complex medical needs of patients results in an elevated patient opinion of the institution's overall quality. In patient-satisfaction surveys, questions regarding the availability of specialists should be incorporated as a *halo effect* for the rest of the medical staff. This also underscores the importance of physician-to-physician relations and the willingness of the administrative staff to find the specialist *stars* of the hospital. Highlighting these physician stars helps to improve the consumer perceptional view of high quality and to influence patient-satisfaction survey responses. Often, these stars can be located through the surveys themselves. Further, by studying the attributes of these providers, it is possible to incorporate the results into training programs to improve the level of quality across the entire staff. This, in turn, will result in improved organizational performance.

Along with consumer views of inferred quality based on the medical staff, patient-satisfaction surveys are influenced by the belief of whether or not the hospital or health system has not only modern equipment but also possibly the best equipment or technology availability. This figures into the complex subjective decision-making process that consumers undertake. It makes sense, then, that if nurses, technical staff, and others are informing patients about the equipment being used to diagnose or treat a specific disease entity, one could assume that quality perceptions would be raised. Patient-satisfaction surveys should include questions regarding the availability, use, and patient assessment of up-to-date technology and equipment. With the easy access and availability of health information in the marketplace, patients better understand the healthcare process and expect nothing but the best. They may not understand the correct treatment uses of the technology and equipment, but they expect them to be available in case they need them.

Courteous employees are another influence on patient-satisfaction levels. We know that patient satisfaction is influenced by the nursing staff's behavior. However, the actions and behavior of the entire staff are constantly being observed and evaluated by patients. As stated earlier, patients view the hospital experience from a perspective of totality, that is, all activities are viewed as the same, not as isolated treatment events. Therefore, from the hospital dietary aides to the CEO, patients expect courteous treatment from every employee. They expect that their questions will be answered, that staff will treat them with dignity and respect, and that the experience will be consistent throughout the hospital. This reinforces the concept that patient satisfaction is the responsibility of everyone and not just the few who provide direct patient care.[39]

Comfort and cleanliness of the patient's surroundings are other important intervening variables in the process of patient satisfaction. Facilities that appear to be new, clean rooms, uncluttered hallways, and well-kept grounds help form the patient's initial impression about the level of competence of the institution and are factors affecting the patient's hospital choice.[13] Carey and Siebert found that comfort and cleanliness ranked in the top five areas of reliability in predicting patient satisfaction.[32]

TABLE 2.1. Levels of Satisfaction with Nurse Courtesy

Category	N	Percentage
Very Satisfied	200	40.0
Somewhat Satisfied	150	30.0
Somewhat Dissatisfied	100	20.0
Very Dissatisfied	50	10.0
Total	500	100.0

This is not to say that if communication skills are improved, physicians are happy, and the physical environment is pleasant, patient-satisfaction scores will automatically improve. As previously noted, patient satisfaction is a complex interwoven set of variables that addresses a patient's total experience of care and must be addressed accordingly. Improvements in these and other areas, however, are very likely to result in improved levels of patient satisfaction.

When surveying patients, it is also important to collect and analyze patient demographic variables. These variables include age, sex, race, ethnicity, income, and so on. Demographic measures provide useful information for understanding the satisfaction process and can provide clues to underlying problem areas. For example, suppose the satisfaction data on nurse courtesy in an outpatient department indicate that 70 percent of patients surveyed are *Very Satisfied* or *Somewhat Satisfied*. Although a 70 percent satisfaction rate may not be cause for general alarm, it is certainly not as high as the administration would like. Table 2.1 displays the distribution of responses to the nurse courtesy question.

Table 2.2 contains the same data broken down by gender. This table clearly indicates that the responses to the question concerning nurse courtesy are strongly affected by the patient's gender.

These data indicate that nearly 87 percent of the women surveyed are satisfied with the courtesy of the nursing staff com-

TABLE 2.2.   Satisfaction with Nurse Courtesy by Gender

Satisfaction Level	Gender		
	Female	Male	
Very Satisfied	150	50	200
Somewhat Satisfied	110	40	150
Somewhat Dissatisfied	30	70	100
Very Dissatisfied	10	40	50
Total	300	200	500

pared to only 45 percent of the male respondents. In fact, if we calculate an appropriate statistical significance test (chi-square), it becomes abundantly clear that the distributions of responses to the question are very different for men and women. The chi-square value for this table is 100.69 with 3 degrees of freedom. This indicates that the satisfaction differences between males and females are statistically significant well beyond the .001 probability level.

What exactly does this tell us about levels of nurse courtesy? It certainly tells us that there are significant problems with the levels of nurse courtesy among men. The next question the hospital's administrators should ask is, *Why do men rate nurse courtesy significantly lower than women?* To address this question, additional research is required. This research may involve focus groups with patients, group meetings with the nursing staff, or some other appropriate strategy designed to get at the root of the problem. Based on the findings of the research, an intervention strategy can be developed and implemented. In this case, one strategy may involve in-house gender-sensitivity training for the staff. Of course, it is imperative that the effects of any interventions be measured to verify changes. A successful intervention should eliminate the gender differences in perceptions of nurse courtesy.

BEFORE, AFTER, AND ONGOING MEASUREMENTS

Measurement is the driving force behind any patient-satisfaction program. As stated earlier, you cannot get to where you want to go unless you know where it is you are going and from where you are beginning. Before and after measurements are the essential ingredients in understanding this process. Additionally, there must be a long-term, continuous organizational commitment to enhancing patient satisfaction. This means that the top executives of the organization must shift their perspectives from a mentality of putting out fires to one of continuous improvement.[39] Patient-satisfaction improvement is not a one-time event. Even though a hospital may become the national benchmark of a given indicator, it does not mean the organization can stop measuring and improving in that area. Patient satisfaction is a continuous process allowing an organization to reach new and higher levels of customer service.

Measurement and analysis provide key information regarding whether the process of satisfaction is in control or out of control, is improving or declining, or whether previous interventions have achieved the desired results. Analysis provides the clues to root causes of problems in the presence of variation.[40] Unanalyzed, raw data cannot provide any indication of the random or variable nature of satisfaction scores. If a process is random, it is unlikely that any intervention will have long-term impact except by chance. For example, analyzing satisfaction data using TQM/SPC methods can determine whether the process is in control or out of control. If out of control, management will be presented with opportunities to gain control by seriously examining the data and developing successful intervention strategies. Once control of the process is gained, management can take appropriate and effective steps to improve patient-satisfaction process levels. As Deming put it,

> "What statistical methods do is to point out the existence of special causes. A point beyond limits on a control chart, or a significant result in an experiment or test, indicates almost certainly the existence of one or more special causes. Points in

control, or showing no significance, indicate that only common causes of variation remain" (p. 97).[40]

Without accurate, timely data that can be processed into useful information, management is left to making decisions based on hunches or gut feelings. Such an approach is unlikely to be successful. As the old saying goes, "In God we trust. All others must use data" (p. 96).[40]

In the coming chapters, we present examples of statistical-process-control charts that indicate at the departmental level where the process of satisfaction is out of control, in control, or improving. This does several things. First, it reveals the randomness and variability in an institution. Essentially, the process of satisfaction is variable from department to department. Second, it shows which departments have begun to address issues surrounding the process of satisfaction. In this case, it becomes necessary for the management team to go back and learn what actions a particular department took to standardize the process of delivering consistent levels of patient satisfaction. Third, the measurements in this example allow investigation of the departments where patient satisfaction is improving. This is necessary to understand how and why they differ from other departments. Replication of success in improving patient satisfaction at the departmental level shortens the length of time it takes to develop lasting interventions across the organization or system.

FINANCIAL IMPLICATIONS

Much has been written about the financial impact of patient satisfaction. Yet it appears that the healthcare community routinely ignores much of this research. In 1992, John Harkey and Robert Vraciu studied the link between quality and financial performance.[34] In the study of HealthTrust hospitals (82 total), they found that a one-standard-deviation change in the quality score represented a 2 percent increase in operating margin. In another study, Eugene Nelson and others found that 17 percent to 27 percent of the variation in hospital profitability could be explained by patient perceptions of quality.[4] Their study examined data on

15,000 patients in 51 Hospital Corporation of America (HCA) hospitals. In addition, Standard and Poor's, the New York bond-rating agency, is investigating how they can incorporate hospital quality indicators into their rating systems.[41] This implies that, in the future, bond rating will be formally influenced by patient-satisfaction data.

One hundred thirty-three hospitals, with a sizable patient-experience database, are being studied to understand the link between profitability, quality, and satisfaction. Being in control and influencing patient satisfaction can have positive financial bottom-line impact. For example, if a hospital's operating margin is 4 percent and patient perceptions of quality can be improved one standard deviation, the margin can improve 2 percent. An upward movement in operating margin from 4 percent to 6 percent results in a significant bottom-line gain of millions of dollars.

This shift can occur for a number of reasons. From a purely marketing viewpoint, a satisfied customer or patient is a loyal customer. By building loyalty to the hospital through positive experiences, future utilization will occur, generating additional revenue. Also, it has been shown that as a loyal user of a facility, a satisfied patient is more likely to positively recommend the institution to others and return for service.[42] This word-of-mouth marketing generates additional utilization, which, in turn, produces revenue to the hospital or system. In many cases, this is new revenue to the hospital or system, because the patient who is referred by word-of-mouth recommendation is in most cases a first-time user.

Quality and process improvements developed under a voice-of-the-customer program utilizing patient-satisfaction data will lead to organizational success. Reductions in length of stay, improved cost efficiencies, and other resulting savings fall to the bottom line and enhance organization performance. Figure 2.1 illustrates what we call the *satisfaction profitability model.* The model illustrates how all the factors we have been discussing interact with one another. By maintaining a base of highly satisfied patients, a healthcare organization can ultimately generate new revenues and higher profit margins and can improve the overall

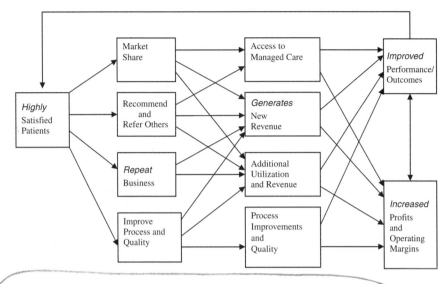

FIGURE 2.1.   Patient-satisfaction Profitability Model

performance of the institution or system. Further, by improving organizational performance and clinical outcomes, patient satisfaction can be further improved.

The concept of patient loyalty as it relates to revenue generation in the satisfaction equation is worth a detailed examination. Although we would not expect dissatisfied patients to be loyal to a healthcare organization, satisfied patients are not automatically loyal patients.[43] A change in a deductible, a more satisfying outcome with another provider, or the recommendation from a family member or friend will cause an individual to change their source of care. Kottler and Clark identified four groups of patients within the loyalty classification. The first group is referred to as *hard-core loyals*. These are individuals who will use your services no matter what. The second group is *soft-core loyals*. Members of this group use two or three different organizations on a regular basis. The third group is termed *shifting loyals*. These are individuals who are in the process of moving to another organization. Finally, the fourth group is referred to as *switchers*, who have no formal allegiance to any organization. The trick, of course, for any healthcare organization is to maintain their base of hard-core loyals and successfully transform members of the other groups.

The financial gain to the institution is that very satisfied loyal patients are repeat users of healthcare services. Therefore, to understand what a loyal patient means to the institution financially, a measure to predict the revenue generation of a loyal patient can be useful. This can be accomplished through measures such as the *repeat-purchase ratio*. By using this measure, it is possible to predict the financial gain to the hospital or system based on patient loyalty. *Loyalty* in this case would be defined as the likelihood that a patient would return for future service. By using this measure, it becomes clear that even a one-point change in loyalty among patients is literally worth millions of dollars. There are several data elements necessary to complete the calculation. First, we need an estimate of the number of the institution's loyal patients. Second, it is important to know and understand their purchase patterns of service within the institution. This would include emergency room, outpatient ancillaries, diagnostic testing, inpatient services, and so forth. Third, we need to know how much revenue is generated by this group. Finally, we need to completely understand why the loyal patients are so satisfied with the services they receive. Their experience, which may appear to be out of the ordinary, needs to be uncovered and replicated to create more loyal patients.

These data elements may be difficult to obtain. Most healthcare organizations do not have very sophisticated data-warehousing systems that allow purchase-behavior patterns of individuals and families to be identified and tracked. Nor have many hospitals or health systems taken the time to understand the concept of loyalty and patient satisfaction to increase repeat business.

An example of how to predict the revenue generated from highly satisfied patients follows. For the sake of argument, assume a hospital ER receives $250 on average per encounter. In this case, for every 100 ER patients, $25,000 in revenue is generated. Not all of these patients are new to or one-time users of the facility. Furthermore, if 50 percent of your ER visits result in admission, the revenue generated is much greater.

Let us also assume that 80 percent of the ER patients have used your healthcare services on other occasions. *Loyalty*, again, is defined as an individual who uses a facility as the sole provider of their healthcare services. We could predict, based on loyalty, that eight in ten patients will be repeat customers. To put it another way, two in ten will be first-time users. Assuming that eight in ten ER visits are made by loyal patients, then, out of 54,000 annual visits, 43,200 will be repeat visits. These 43,200 encounters times the average revenue of $250 per encounter equals nearly $11 million in potential revenue (not including additional inpatient revenue). That leaves 10,000 visits from potential first-time users, which generates another $2.5 million. This implies that even a small percentage increase in the number of loyal customers results in potentially sizable revenue increases.

In any market, volume is generated by repeat business. There are simply not enough patients available to turn over entire markets among healthcare providers. Calculation of the repeat-purchase ratio for your hospital or health system will confirm this fact. Yet, marketing strategies commonly concentrate on acquiring new customers, when, clearly, revenue is driven in large part by repeat business. Few organizations engage in customer-retention strategies, which would provide a larger payoff in terms of resources expended. It is much easier to keep a current customer than to find new customers. The cost of recruiting new patients is five times greater than retaining current patients.[28] Again, satisfaction becomes a critical element in the continued success of your business. Through patient satisfaction, you may be able to find strategies to increase the level of loyalty among current users, generating repeat business and revenue.

Can you infer loyalty from patient-satisfaction data? In a recent article, Drachman examined this concept using a database comprised of 11,000 adult inpatients.[44] Survey data were collected from 27 academic health centers, which are part of the University Health System Consortium. The scale used was the 28 report-type items from the Picker Institute adult inpatient questionnaire. Drachman examined a number of reported patient responses to the question, *Would you recommend this hospital to your family and friends?* This is a common question used by many third-party satisfaction-data-collection companies. Patient-satisfaction data can be used as a proxy measure for loyalty. Some inferences can be made, but detailed understanding and analysis are needed to truly understand why one patient is loyal and another is not.

It is possible to view the healthcare encounter in a hospital as a sales transaction involving the provision of a service. As such, the quality of the transaction viewed by the patient is expressed as satisfaction with the process and will help determine loyalty to the institution. Loyalty brings repeat business, as well as new business through word-of-mouth referrals. Being able to calculate a loyalty quotient allows administrators to predict, with some certainty, the effect of patient satisfaction on the bottom line.

Some may argue that the process of healthcare is not the same as a monetary transaction like buying a refrigerator. On the contrary, with the growth of managed care and the reemergence of consumer choice, healthcare has entered the free-market arena. By being able to buy, sell, and obtain healthcare from a variety of providers, healthcare in essence has become a commodity. Hence, patient satisfaction is of growing importance as a method to gain financial advantages and can differentiate an institution in a very crowed market. Loyalty, operating margin, and new revenue can be achieved and sustained through a carefully understood and managed patient-satisfaction program.

SUMMARY

Improving patient satisfaction across the organization or system has major implications for the overall performance of a healthcare organization.[45] It is clear that understanding the links between satisfaction levels, patient loyalty, and outcome measures is key to a healthcare organization's success. Committing to a program dedicated to improving satisfaction levels will result in more than having happy customers; it will result in a healthier financial position. This commitment must be long-term, and it must be embraced by the entire organization.

Chapter 3

PATIENT-SATISFACTION SURVEY AUDIT

QUALITY DECISIONS REQUIRE QUALITY DATA

Making meaningful quality and cost improvements requires high-quality, valid, and reliable data. *Validity* refers to whether questions or the data-collection instruments actually measure what they are intended to measure. *Reliability* refers to whether the questions or the instruments measure the same thing each time they are used. Validity ensures reliability, but a reliable instrument is not necessarily valid. That is, a question or an instrument may be measuring the same thing each time it is used, but it may not be measuring what it is intended to measure. Obviously, when it comes to using patient-satisfaction data for improving the quality of care an organization provides, both issues are key. Carey and Seibert provide a good overview of validity and reliability issues related to patient-satisfaction data collection, as well as a strategy for measuring both.[32]

Data used in quality improvement programs usually come from a variety of sources and provide the organization with a comprehensive view of its performance. Some data may come from areas of internal operation, such as finance, decision support, risk management, quality improvement, and medical records. Generalized data are available from third-party reports, benchmark performance data found in trade publications, or from white-paper reports.

Quality improvement data typically come from severity-adjustment systems, such as HCIA or HBSI. An important source of data often overlooked in many quality improvement programs, however, is patient-satisfaction data. Satisfaction data combined with a voice-of-the-customer program can significantly improve a hospital's cost and quality position in the market.

To make quality decisions regarding improvement strategies, it is imperative that the data used to make such decisions is high quality. The old data-processing adage of *garbage in–garbage out (GIGO)* is relevant and applicable to using patient-satisfaction data for quality and performance improvement. Currently, it is common for healthcare organizations to outsource patient-satisfaction data collection to third-party, proprietary organizations. As a convenience, a nonexhaustive list of organizations specializing in patient-satisfaction data collection and analysis services is provided in Appendix A. Reasons for outsourcing the data collection are usually related to cost, convenience, and organizational competence. That is, some healthcare organizations feel it is less expensive to outsource than to maintain a qualified staff of survey and statistical experts. Others may feel that receiving satisfaction data from a proprietary organization on a regular basis is convenient and reduces nonclinical functions within the institution. Still others may feel they do not have the necessary level of competence within the organization to carry out the tasks associated with collecting their own patient-satisfaction data.

Even if a healthcare organization outsources its patient-satisfaction data-collection process, it would be unwise to haphazardly select a company without considering several key factors. Just because a company is in the business of collecting data for hospitals and other healthcare organizations does not automatically ensure that they provide a quality product. Before selecting any data-collection company, issues surrounding the following questions should be satisfactorily addressed:

- Is the data-collection instrument valid and reliable?
- What specific questions are asked?
- How is the patient sample drawn?

- How large is the sample?
- Who is responsible for drawing the sample?
- To what organizations will you be compared?
- What benchmarking is used?
- What is the size of the database from which comparisons are made?

THE PATIENT-SATISFACTION SURVEY CHECKLIST/AUDIT

The main purpose of the following checklist is to help determine whether the organization is moving in the right direction in the measurement of patient satisfaction. This review should assist in answering questions related to whether the hospital or health system is performing optimally and is realizing the accomplishment of its goals and objectives relative to patient satisfaction. The audit should provide a clear understanding of the strengths and weaknesses of the current system and pinpoints areas for improvement. Thus, we have developed a checklist that can be employed to answer critical organizational questions about the patient-satisfaction data-collection process. In the end, the checklist should provide a reasonable sense of the quality of the process used and how to do a better job of data collection.

This audit focuses on several key areas that must be reviewed periodically. Changing patient populations, market conditions, and service configurations need to be reflected in any ongoing measurement efforts. The major areas that need to be constantly reviewed are the type of survey, the survey questions, the data-collection method, the issues of question validity and reliability, statistical reliability, benchmarks, data analysis, data utilization, cost, and the support services provided by the satisfaction vendor.

When used properly, the checklist/audit can serve several purposes. First, the list represents a comprehensive set of questions that can be used as an evaluation tool. Whether the management team is asking these questions about its own in-house process or about an external patient-satisfaction data-collection organization,

Survey Audit Guide		
1. Is the Survey		
	Yes	No
• An in-house creation?		
• From a patient-satisfaction survey vendor?		
2. What types of surveys do you participate in?		
Each area requires separate questionnaires and may require different data-collection strategies. For each relevant area, does the current or proposed data-collection process cover those services provided by the organization?		
	Yes	No
• Inpatient services		
• Outpatient services		
• Emergency room		
• Ambulatory care center		
• Home health		
• Long-term care		
• Physician office		
• Surgi-center		
3. Survey questions		
Are major aggregate scales in the following areas provided?		
The following measures are required to obtain a good overall view of how well the organization is performing.		
	Yes	No
• Total facility medical outcome		
• Physician-satisfaction scale		

	Yes	No
• Nursing-satisfaction scale		
• Admission/discharge		
• Food service		
• Housekeeping		
• Ancillary department satisfaction		
• Other staff courtesy		
• Facilities/plant operations		
Are aggregate results of the individual items trended against the previous period?		
• Two previous periods?		
• Three previous periods?		
Are questions of loyalty and future use asked?		
• Would you return to this facility for care?		
• Would you recommend this facility to another person?		
Do you have the ability to modify the survey through question addition or deletion?		
Are demographics collected?		
Breaking satisfaction data down by demographic categories allows the management team to locate and rectify problems affecting specific subgroups of the general patient population.		
	Yes	No
• Age		
• Sex		
• Race		

	Yes	No
• Payer type		
• Income		
• Occupation		
• Household size		
• Frequency of visit		
• Discharge diagnosis		
• Nursing unit stay		

The following information is used to tie patient satisfaction to other areas of organizational performance by making comparisons over time.

	Yes	No
Can you compare satisfaction results against overall financial reports?		
Can you compare satisfaction results to outcome measures?		
Can you compare satisfaction results for a new patient versus results for a previous patient?		
If a member of a multihospital system, do all members use the same survey instrument?		
Do the individual survey scale questions provide comparative benchmarks		

	Yes	No
Are those results trended against the previous survey periods?		
• The previous period?		
• Two surveys ago?		
• Three surveys ago?		
• Long-term comparisons?		

4. What data-collection method do you use?

	Yes	No
• Mail		
• Telephone		
• Exit/discharge		
• Point of service		
• Patient bedside		

The following items relate to issues surrounding response rates, efficiency, and analytic capabilities.

	Yes	No
Can the survey responses be scanned into a computer program?		
Can patients enter survey answers via your Internet site?		
Can patients enter data via interactive telephone methods?		
What percentage of patients receives surveys?		
How are those patients chosen?		
What is the response rate?		

	Yes	No
Does the sample represent the demographics of the hospital?		
Can your sampling systems flag patients not to receive multiple surveys?		
Can your sampling system exclude deceased patients?		
If a mail survey, is the survey self-addressed for ease of return?		
Is the survey coded for identification?		
Can you identify patients for follow-up?		
5. Questions relating to validity and reliability		
	Yes	No
Are the questions independent of one another? (That is, if nursing improves, does it improve because of an improvement in nursing and not with physician care?)		
What statistical tests have the questions and survey been subjected to for result verification?		
	Yes	No
Have the questions been assigned weights in the analysis process?		
What are those weights, and how were they determined?		

	Yes	No
Are the questions constantly reviewed by the provider for appropriateness?		
Are new survey questions pretested prior to inclusion in the survey?		
Have the statistical testing results been subjected to peer-review mechanisms for publication on the effectiveness of the survey?		
6. Statistical reliability		
What is the level of statistical confidence?		
What is the level of external and internal reliability?		
What statistical significance tests has the survey been subjected to?		

	Yes	No
• t-test		
• Chi-square		
• Standard error of the mean		
• Standard error percentage		
• Cronbach's alpha		
Have any published articles appeared about the survey and its statistical reliability?		
Have any articles appeared about the survey at all?		
Against what size of patient database is the survey measured?		

7. Comparative benchmarks

	Yes	No
Can you select the benchmark hospitals for comparison that reflect your size, geographic location, and payer mix?		
Can you compare your facility to best practice in the database?		
Can you contact the best-practice facility?		
How often is the comparative database updated?		

	Yes	No
• Annually		
• Semiannually		
• Quarterly		
Are there user group meetings with member case studies for presentation?		
Is there a website to go to and share information?		

8. Data analysis

What types of vendor analysis reports are available?		
What types of data analysis are routinely provided?		

	Yes	No
• Frequency distributions		
• Rasch analysis		

	Yes	No
• Group comparisons		
• Regression analysis		
• Analysis of variance (ANOVA)		
• Factor analysis		
Can you custom-design reports?		
Can you obtain the raw data for additional analysis?		
Can reports be provided in TQM formats?		
Are internal reports and summaries provided?		
Can the data be linked to financial results?		
Can the data be linked to outcome studies?		
How many internal full-time equivalents (FTEs) are devoted to the patient-satisfaction process?		
How are survey results processed by the organization?		
What ongoing support does the vendor provide for detailed analysis?		
9. Data utilization		
How are the reports utilized in the organization?		
How are the benefits of satisfaction measured?		

How are goals for patient-satisfaction improvement established?		
How are results communicated to employees?		
The board of directors?		
Physicians?		
Employers?		
Managed-care companies?		
How are reports communicated to the community?		
	Yes	No
Are satisfaction results used in employee evaluations?		
Are satisfaction reports used in a report-card format?		
10. Cost		
How much does the current survey method cost?		
What is the ongoing maintenance cost?		
	Yes	No
Are you planning to add surveys?		
How long is the contract for?		
	Yes	No
Is the contract self-renewing?		
Is there a more cost-efficient method to collect data?		

	Yes	No
Does the cost of administration justify the returns?		
Have you allocated sufficient dollars for an effective satisfaction measurement program?		
Have you recently completed the request-for-proposals (RFP) process to ensure best possible cost efficiency?		
Have you determined what the costs of not doing satisfaction surveys are?		
11. Vendor support services		
What types of vendor support services are available?		
What processes does the vendor use to ensure data-input accuracy?		
What types of staff training and support are available?		
	Yes	No
Do you take advantage of all the services included in your contract?		
Does the vendor produce a monthly or bimonthly newsletter?		
Does the vendor publish a directory of survey-participating hospitals or systems?		
Does the vendor have the ability to scan surveys in the processing system?		

	Yes	No
Will the vendor make presentations to the organization?		
Is reporting software available?		
Does the vendor have data-consulting programs available?		
Does the vendor have a customer-satisfaction program?		
Does the vendor have a voice-of-the-customer program?		
Does the vendor support TQM/CQI programs?		

process deficiencies can be identified and corrected. Second, the questions can be used to guide a request-for-proposals (RFP) or request-for-information (RFI) process. In the process of soliciting information from patient-satisfaction vendors, using these questions provides a relatively exhaustive and standardized set of criteria for comparative purposes. Third, once proposals have been submitted, the question set provides a mechanism to evaluate and rank vendors. Doing so provides valuable information to assist in the decision-making process.

OUTSOURCING THE SURVEY USING MAIL OR TELEPHONE: PLUSES AND MINUSES

Collecting usable patient-satisfaction data is not inexpensive. To improve quality and customer perceptions, high-quality data are required. As noted in the audit, there are several data-collection strategies that can be employed to gather patient-satisfaction data. Each approach has both positive and negative aspects. The strategy employed depends on the individual organization's needs, the resources available to devote to the patient-satisfaction process, and methodological considerations. To assist in the process, we have summarized the pluses and minuses of each category of data-collection approach. A key criterion to consider in all methods is the response rate. The *response rate* is calculated as

$$RR = \frac{\text{Number of usable questionnaires completed}}{\text{Number of questionnaires distributed}} \times 100$$

and is expressed as a percentage. Obviously, the goal is to have the highest response rate possible. In general, response rates for all surveys have been declining. An intensive follow-up of all non-respondents can help bolster sagging response rates. Such follow-up programs, however, can be very expensive.

Mail Surveys

Using mail surveys can be the most cost effective and reliable method to collect patient-satisfaction information. Response rates should generally be in the 50 percent range. Major costs in conducting a mail survey include the printing of the survey, the printing of a cover letter, postage, survey return postage, follow-up reminder letters or postcards after the first mailing, and a second mailing letter and survey for a portion of the original sample. Staff time is needed for the process as well. Time must be allocated for assembling the cover letter and survey, addressing the envelope package, mailing the package, compiling return surveys, and preparing the responses for analysis. Information system time is also required to generate a random sample of patients to be surveyed, their addresses, and the labels. In terms of full-time equivalents, upwards of 40 hours per survey period will be required to successfully complete the process. Regular reports should be generated by third-party vendors for distribution within the institution. If the survey is being conducted in-house, resources necessary to generate reports should also be considered.

Pluses for this type of survey include:

- Hospital control of process
- Costs limited to printing, postage, and staff time to administer survey

- Reliable results
- Ongoing investment that can be constant and predictable for budget
- Surveys that can be customized without much effort
- Large database for benchmark comparisons
- Actionable results within acceptable statistical variance

Minuses include:

- Intensive internal staff effort to prepare surveys for distribution
- Loss of control of individual questionnaires once they are mailed
- Functional illiteracy rate in the United States that hovers around 10 percent to 12 percent
- No opportunity for homeless patients to respond
- Possibility of foreign-language-speaking patients not being able to respond
- Variation in return rates given population being sampled
- Lag time of results reporting from 30 to 60 days postsurvey
- Need for surveys to be reprinted if survey changes, increasing costs
- Postal increases that can negatively affect budget
- Potential error for majority of responses by one particular demographic group
- Staff departures in survey process that stop or delay timing of survey

Telephone Interviews

The main differences between a mail approach and using the telephone are obvious. Using a telephone rather than the mail as the delivery mechanism means that an interviewer is necessary to ask the questions once a respondent is contacted. Interviewers are useful because they can circumvent the illiteracy problem, they can establish a sense of personal relationship, and they can assist the respondent if the questions are unclear.

Pluses for this type of survey include:

- Immediate response and feedback in survey period
- Relatively fast process
- Easy and inexpensive callbacks
- Greater response rate
- No staff time involved in data collection
- Standard questions available
- Sample size and response by demographic group controllable
- Reliable statistical results
- Large comparative benchmark database
- Actionable reports and results

Minuses include:

- More costly option than mail surveys to obtain patient-satisfaction survey information
- Customized questions available but at a premium price
- Patients receiving phone calls perceiving it as intrusive
- Inconsistent phone presentations
- Some patients without telephones (rates vary by geographic location)
- Multiple telephone numbers, which may mean calling the same patient several times
- Multiple callbacks to obtain response
- Results difficult to compare to other survey methods if change is implemented
- Comparative databases unavailable for customized questions

Point-of-Service Strategies

Point-of-service strategies include exit or discharge surveys, bed-side surveys, or surveying patients at any time during the visit or stay. These data-collection approaches are relatively simple for institutions to implement in-house, but, if done on a large scale, they can become complicated.

Pluses of POS strategies include:

- Immediate feedback
- Ability of patient to enter information via kiosk or computer terminal
- Problems and concerns presented immediately addressed
- Cost effective due to patient doing the work/little direct staff involvement
- Reports computer generated from database
- Easy to change or add questions
- Can be ongoing method to acquire information
- Computer software easily updated
- Data continuously being collected

Minuses include:

- Data continuously being collected
- Responses to the questions that may be biased due to the patient's condition
- Possible patient perception of a lack of confidentiality and/or anonymity
- Usually involve nonprobability samples, making generalizations difficult
- Initial cost of POS system high
- No comparative database available
- No method to control respondents, resulting in oversampling of one population
- Possibility of patients responding more than once during a stay
- Results possibly subject to a *white-coat* effect
- Results possibly not statistically reliable
- Patients possibly fearful of computers
- Potential problems of safeguarding electronic information

The method by which an organization chooses to conduct patient-satisfaction surveys will be based upon cost, the organization's philosophy toward satisfaction, and how the results will be used internally. All three approaches have pluses and minuses. The best option is the one that the hospital or health system feels most comfortable with, best meets its unique needs, and best taps the information of its patient population.

SUMMARY

There are many key factors to consider when establishing or modifying a patient-satisfaction data-collection program. Always remember the garbage in–garbage out adage. Quality improvement strategies based on poor data have little chance of success. Maximizing the quality of the patient-satisfaction data you collect maximizes the chances of successfully improving your organization's performance. Periodically reviewing your data-collection program using the checklist/audit will result in improved data and, ultimately, improved decision making.

Chapter 4

PATIENT-SATISFACTION TQM/CQI PROCESS STRATEGIES

INTRODUCTION

This chapter focuses on statistical-process-control (SPC) methods that can be applied to patient-satisfaction data. We examine the following six SPC tools:

1. Checksheets
2. Histograms
3. Pareto charts
4. Cause-and-effect diagrams (fishbone diagrams)
5. Scatter diagrams
6. Control charts

By applying each of these methods to patient-satisfaction data, problem areas can be highlighted and clues as to the solutions to problems can be uncovered. For each tool, we provide an example of its use as related to patient-satisfaction data. Although there are a number of specialized computer software packages available that specifically focus on CQI measurement tools, all of our examples have been created using Microsoft Office 97™. Our purpose is to show how Word™, Excel™, and Power Point™ can be adapted to these applications. We have elected to use these products because they are so widely used throughout the industry. This means that new software may be unnecessary in many situations, and resources should not be required for training.

Before discussing the measurement tools, it is important to understand why it is imperative to pay close attention to patient-satisfaction data. Our view is that patient-satisfaction data provide valuable insight into the voice of the customer and the voice of the process, both of which are integral to enhancing clinical and financial performance.

VOICE OF THE CUSTOMER

Over the course of the past decade, the customer has emerged as a driving force behind the changes being experienced in the healthcare industry. Today's consumer is better informed, demands higher product quality, and expects personalized service delivery, along with service excellence. The information age has allowed consumers to easily and cheaply gain access to the increasingly expanding healthcare knowledge base. The obvious result is that patients have become savvy purchasers of healthcare services, often demanding greater decision-making power in their relationships with providers. The less obvious result is that healthcare administrators, physicians, nurses, and other ancillary healthcare professionals must change the ways they do their jobs. Heightened sensitivity to the patient's needs and demands is required. Approaching patient care in the traditional manner will result in elevated levels of patient dissatisfaction. Additionally, patients will voice their dissatisfaction with the institution's delivery of care through the survey process. Ultimately, in a competitive environment, patients will voice their concerns by choosing another provider.

The *voice of the customer*, commonly referred to as *VOC*, should be a formal mechanism within the organization utilizing quantitative and qualitative measures to gain greater knowledge about the customer.[6] Often, the VOC is the least understood component of the TQM process. Consider the analogy to a spoked wheel. At the hub of the wheel is the individual patient. Emanating from the hub are three spokes connecting to the rim of the wheel, forming a solid circle. The three spokes in the wheel represent parameters delimiting sections within the wheel. The sections represent management areas within the institution related to process improvement, strategic planning, and product development. Although they are often viewed as separate areas, they are interconnected and interrelated with the customer at the center of the process. An organization's quality improvement efforts, long- and short-range planning, and product-development cycles are driven by the knowledge gained from listening and responding to the voice of the customer.

For a quality function deployment (QFD)* team to work efficiently and effectively, for example, they must use a VOC process. An underlying principle of TQM is to include customer input as a means to improve quality.[40] Patient-satisfaction data provide this critical input. Past efforts within the industry have focused on making decisions based on internal operations data. Through searching out and discovering best-practice organizations, process improvements in healthcare have been internalized. As a result, patients, as consumers of care, benefited indirectly. Management used internal operational data to focus on issues related to reducing costs, more efficiently using available resources, lowering lengths of stay, downsizing staff, and so on. Considerably less effort or attention has been directed toward measuring patient satisfaction.

Patient-satisfaction information is a key component of the VOC process and must be viewed that way. Satisfaction data reflect customer perceptions of how well the organization is doing and provide valuable clues about how to improve. To become truly focused on patient perceptions, the routine measurement of patient satisfaction should be merged with the VOC process. Patient-satisfaction data represent a key element in organizational growth. Figure 4.1 illustrates how the VOC can be used in relation to improvements in the organizational infrastructure.

---

*QFD teams are also referred to as quality improvement teams, deployment teams, or process improvement teams.[23]

Flowchart

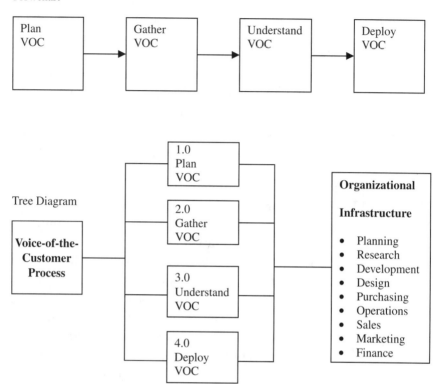

FIGURE 4.1. Voice-of-the-Customer Process and Organizational Infrastructure. The VOC Process is shown as a Flowchart and a Tree Diagram

Reprinted with permission from GOAL/QPC, *The Memory Jogger*™ (2 Manor Parkway, Salem, N.H., 1988).

Patient satisfaction becomes a primary driving force in the VOC process. As data are collected in all departments and resulting changes are deployed across the organization, the focus shifts dramatically to the customer. This shift is necessary to create an organizational culture of satisfaction. Ultimately, information garnered from patient-satisfaction data reflects both the voice of the customer and the voice of the process.

VOICE OF THE PROCESS

Process is the mechanism by which a task or a series of tasks is accomplished in order to achieve a predetermined goal or objective.[40] In healthcare, this could be the way a patient is admitted to the hospital, how radiology schedules and provides outpatient services, or how patient-satisfaction data are collected. When processes work as intended and produce the desired results, the organization runs smoothly. When processes fail, however, the outcomes are increased cost, rework, waste, and dissatisfied customers.

Patient-satisfaction surveys query individuals on key elements of organizational processes. For example, a typical survey question asks the respondent about the level of communication between the nurse and the patient regarding the care plan or critical pathway. This question assumes several things. First, it assumes that the process was correctly implemented. Second, it assumes that there was sufficient and adequate communication among all the departments involved in developing the patient's care plan, enabling the nurse to effectively communicate with the patient, family, or significant others. Finally, it assumes that the patient had specific knowledge concerning the process and was an active participant the process. Thus, when the patient reports dissatisfaction with the nurse's communication, it may reflect more on the total process of care than on the individual nurse.

The *voice of the process (VOP)* is uncovered by examining patient responses to the questionnaire. It is important, therefore, to include survey questions that tap elements of the process. This enables the QFD team to design and implement quality improvement strategies by responding to the VOC and the VOP.

A relevant aspect of the VOP is that patients' views of their healthcare experiences represent a set of interrelated events and processes. For example, a complaint about cold food may actually summarize more serious organizational problems. Perhaps the food was delivered while the patient was away from the room for tests. Nursing and dietary should have interacted to make arrangements to hold the food for a later time. Thus, dissatisfaction with the food may uncover a serious process flaw, namely lack of communication within the organization.

By examining the VOP, process flaws can be detected and corrected. The first step toward uncovering process flaws is to measure and analyze the VOC and the VOP. To do so, TQM analysis tools become invaluable when applied to patient-satisfaction data. Their intelligent use will result in a patient-centered organization and improvements in quality.

ANALYSIS TOOLS TO MEASURE, DIAGNOSE, AND CONTROL THE PROCESS
Checksheets

In production management situations, *checksheets* are often used to examine the distribution of defective parts.[46] For use with patient-satisfaction data, checksheets can be used to identify the frequency of occurrence of particular items related to the process of care. For example, many facilities have established a method of collecting complaints about various aspects of service delivery. When these complaints, representing patient dissatisfaction, are collected, a checksheet provides a strategy to compile the responses into a usable format. Checksheets provide tallies for different categories of dissatisfaction. Figure 4.2 provides an example of a checksheet analyzing patient complaints. (This checksheet was created using Microsoft Word™ by invoking some of the elements located in the *Drawing Toolbar.*)

The checksheet contains the different major categories of patients' complaints. As the complaints are read, a check mark is placed in the appropriate category. When completed, the number of checks within each category of complaint is totaled, resulting in a frequency distribution. Checksheets should be developed on an ongoing basis. In this case, for example, the checksheet for patient complaints is compiled every month. Doing so creates a picture of patient dissatisfaction over time and allows for an examination of the effects of management interventions.

Patient Complaints

Date: June 1999

Complaint Category	Checks	Subtotal
Waiting Time Too Long	⫫⫫ ⫫⫫ ⫫⫫ ⫫⫫ ⫫⫫ ///	28
Discourteous Staff	⫫⫫ ⫫⫫ ⫫⫫ ///	18
Facility Cleanliness	⫫⫫ ⫫⫫ ⫫⫫ ⫫⫫ ⫫⫫ ⫫⫫ /	31
Other	⫫⫫ ⫫⫫ //	12
	Total	89

FIGURE 4.2.   Checksheet of Patient Complaints

As in any industry, customer complaints can serve as a catalyst for improvement. For example, the checksheet in the figure indicates that 28 complaints have been received concerning excessive waiting times to receive diagnostic tests over a 4-day period. Based on these data, managers should raise several questions about the process. For example:

1. Was the delay related to one particular department?
2. What were the *scheduled* patient loads compared to the *actual* loads?
3. Was there any unusual trauma activity or an increase in emergent referrals by physicians?
4. Did the equipment require any unscheduled maintenance?
5. Were staffing levels (physician, nursing, and technical) sufficient to handle the volume?
6. Was a block or modified scheduling system in place?

The management team needs to determine whether the unusually high number of complaints reflects a flaw in the system, an anomaly, or whether patients have begun to *game* the system. When we refer to *gaming the system,* we mean that patients may have learned that nothing happens on time, so they arrive early hoping to be treated by their original appointment time. Such patient behavior may have the effect of shifting the facility's scheduling system from a priority discipline to a first-come, first-served system, which, in turn, may further decrease patient-satisfaction levels.

The checksheet has given the management team the first of many clues that there may be a problem with the CQI process by illuminating a problem area. Managers should routinely review these cases to determine the sources of the problem and what, if any, intervention is required to solve the problem. One compelling technique is to ask the question *Why?* five times. Each time an answer is given, it is met with another *Why?* Usually, by the fifth round, everyone has a basic understanding of the process and why the problem occurred.[47] Another strategy might be to use a *nominal group technique* to develop a cause-and-effect diagram.[48]

The management team can trace the source of the problem to a lack of communication between the staff and the patients. Simple communication, such as explaining the reason for a delay to patients and offering of assistance, can ease the negative perceptions of waiting time. As an intervention strategy, the management team might decide to develop a program of using volunteers as conversational hosts to provide patients with a friendly face and a friendly ear during the wait. In addition, hospital staff could be reminded of the importance of overtly friendly gestures when dealing with patients. Smiling more, showing concern for the patient, and indicating understanding of the patient's situation, along with providing regular updates, all help the waiting time go faster. On those rare occasions when the delay is due to unforeseen circumstances, free meal passes redeemable in the hospital cafeteria or some other goodwill gesture could be provided.

After implementing any new program, the management team must evaluate the results by closely monitoring complaints and by thoroughly reviewing the results of the patient-satisfaction surveys. If the problem is not corrected, they must repeat the process. It is important to remember that this is a continuous, cyclical process, not a onetime effort.

TABLE 4.1. Patients' Satisfaction With Most Recent Visit

Satifaction Level	f	Percentage
Very Satisfied	190	32.4
Somewhat Satisfied	298	50.7
Somewhat Dissatisfied	59	10.0
Very Dissatisfied	41	6.9
Total	598	100.0

Histograms

Histograms, sometimes referred to as *bar charts*, represent a way to graphically display frequency distributions. *Frequency distributions* are tabulations of responses into grouped categories. For example, suppose we survey patients and ask the question, *How satisfied overall were you with your most recent visit to our facility?*, with response choices of *Very Satisfied, Somewhat Satisfied, Somewhat Dissatisfied, and Very Dissatisfied*. We tabulate the responses to the question by counting the number of answers falling into each response category. This results in the creation of a frequency distribution. Table 4.1 contains the distribution of responses to this question based on a total of 587 completed patient-satisfaction questionnaires.

After calibrating the responses, we can proceed with the development of a histogram. The histogram often makes the nature of the frequency distribution clearer. A histogram is fundamentally an *x-y* graph with the response categories forming the baseline (horizontal) or *x* axis, and the frequency delineating the vertical or *y* axis. The frequency can be displayed either as raw numbers or as the percentage of total responses. Figure 4.3 illustrates a histogram showing the percentage distribution of responses to the question of satisfaction with the patients' most recent visit. The frequency associated with each response category is represented by a bar on the graph. (This graph was developed

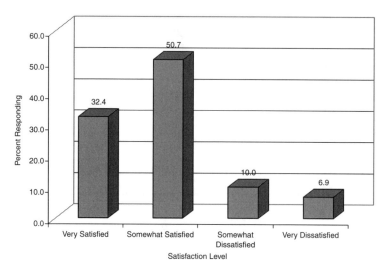

FIGURE 4.3.   Satisfaction With Most Recent Visit Histogram

by creating a spreadsheet in Microsoft Excel™ and creating a
graph using the *Bar Graph* option.)

The histogram provides the QFD with a visual scan of the
patient-satisfaction information for this item while providing
clues to prioritizing problem resolution. As can be seen from the
histogram in Figure 4.3, patients report being generally satisfied
with their recent visit overall. However, only around 30 percent
of the respondents report being *Very Satisfied*. Additionally,
around 50 percent report being *Somewhat Satisfied* with their visit.
Although a 20 percent dissatisfaction rate may not be an immediate cause for alarm, it does indicate that a sizable proportion of
the facility's patients are less than overjoyed with the totality of
their healthcare experience. From a purely marketing standpoint,
the QFD team should realize that these dissatisfied patients are
unlikely to make referrals to others through word of mouth.

It is a common practice to combine the *Very Satisfied* category
with the *Somewhat Satisfied* category to arrive at an 80 percent satisfaction rate. The danger with this approach is that basic problems can be overlooked. This type of TQM tool shows the man-

agement team that there is an overall problem and at what levels the problem exists. After examining all response categories separately, they may be collapsed for convenience and ease of interpretation. Subsequently, solutions to the problem can be developed and implemented. As a visual cue, histograms can be used facility-wide as an illustration of important change concepts. Comparing histograms over time (i.e., from quarter to quarter) provides evidence of the positive effects of managerial interventions. Ideally, the facility will see a steady movement upward in the *Very Satisfied* category.

Pareto Charts

Pareto charts are similar to histograms in form but differ in function in a couple of ways. First, Pareto charts typically graph single responses to multiple items rather than multiple responses to single items. Second, the response categories are displayed in order of decreasing frequency or importance. Figure 4.4 illustrates the use of a Pareto chart to examine negative responses to a series of five satisfaction questions, which form a composite index relating to the patient's rating of the level of comfort and cleanliness of the hospital and the hospital room. These questions relate to:

1. The cleanliness of the room (7 percent)
2. The temperature of the room (19 percent)
3. The general cleanliness of the hospital (2 percent)
4. The courtesy of the housekeeping staff (4 percent)
5. The patient's overall opinion of the housekeeping staff (3 percent)

Respondents were asked to rate these features of the hospital stay with possible response choices of *Excellent, Good, Fair,* or *Poor.* In this case, because of small numbers, the *Fair* and *Poor* categories are combined. The number in parentheses after each item presented in the preceding list represents the percentage of respondents answering *Fair* or *Poor.* (Figure 4.4 was created using Microsoft Excel™ in the same manner as the histogram.)

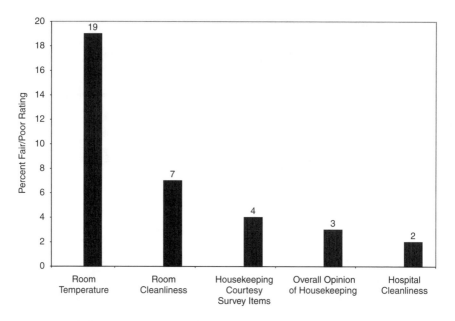

FIGURE 4.4.   Percentage of Resondents Answering *Fair/Poor* to Comfort and Courtesy Items Pareto Chart

Management teams collect considerable amounts of data on patient satisfaction as part of their evaluation processes. A primary advantage to using TQM tools as part of the process is that they provide an effective way to organize considerable amounts of data. In this case, the QFD team has compiled data on the inpatient experience as related to environmental issues. By arranging the data in descending order of importance, the team can obtain a visual confirmation of the relative impact of the hotel functions (including hospitality and guest relations) of the facility on the patients' perceptions about their inpatient stay. From these data, it is clear that room temperature is the most immediate problem requiring intervention.

Often, it is impossible to solve all problems simultaneously. In fact, it is often suggested that interventions be directed at the most urgent problem(s) first.[40,46] After implementing the intervention, a new Pareto chart is developed and the process repeated. In the example illustrated in Figure 4.4, it is clear that improvements in the comfort and courtesy elements can be directed at two different areas, physical plant and housekeeping.

The QFD team, working together with the housekeeping staff and plant operations, should further investigate the problem and search for solutions. First, the team must compile identical analyses for different areas of the facility. This will allow them to determine if the issue is facility-wide or if it occurs only in isolated areas. Next, in collaboration with the physical plant staff, the QFD team should seek answers to the following set of questions regarding room temperatures:

1. What is the repair history of the thermostats in the affected rooms?
2. Do the affected rooms have excessive or unusual sun exposure that might increase room temperature? Does a lack of sun make the rooms colder?
3. Are patients opening windows?
4. What is the process of problem reports to plant operations? Are there any obvious flaws in the process?
5. Are patients reporting problems as they occur?

A similar strategy can be employed with the housekeeping staff. The QFD team strategy must reemphasize the importance of the housekeeping function to the hospital's overall success.

Pareto charts provide information for implementing rapid change. The management team is able to prioritize problem areas and assist in developing the process-related questions that enable the team to focus on key issues and to develop a resolution strategy.

Cause-and-Effect Diagrams

The *cause-and-effect diagram* is a quality improvement tool that enables the deconstruction of organizational problems into smaller component parts with the goal of finding their root causes. Often this technique is used in conjunction with a *nominal group technique*. The nominal group technique involves bringing organizational experts and stakeholders together to solve a problem.[48]

When examining patient-satisfaction issues, the cause-and-effect diagram can provide valuable feedback on the *four Ms* of management: manpower, methods, materials, and mechanicals.[6] These provide an effective way to compartmentalize the care process, which allows management to focus on specific causal areas. Patient satisfaction is a complex process measured by a complex set of variables, which, taken together, represent the totality of the patient experience. This means that patients often do not view their healthcare experience as isolated events of diagnosis and treatment. That is, subjective judgments and evaluations are not based on the actions of individual departments but on the interaction among departments. Poor evaluations of one component of the overall healthcare experience are often generalized to the entire facility. Thus, the importance of the four Ms as areas of focus within the cause-and-effect framework is that they allow an examination of all aspects of the process of service delivery.

The cause-and-effect diagram is a visual tool that assists management in establishing the root causes of a problem. To begin, the problem under investigation becomes the *effect* and the four Ms represent areas of potential *causes*. Figure 4.5 illustrates a general case example of the starting point for developing the diagram. (This diagram was created using Microsoft Power Point™ but could also be developed using Microsoft Word™.)

To make the example patient-satisfaction specific, the team must first select the quality issue (satisfaction problem area) that they would like to improve. Next, the team needs to focus on the four Ms (causes) of the problem area. Each category is portrayed as a branch off the main "backbone" of the diagram. Within each of these causal categories, more specific possible causes are delineated and added to the diagram. These are subsequently added to the diagram as additional branches off each of the main branches representing the four Ms and represent subcauses of the problem.

The cause-and-effect diagram is set up in a manner similar to the one in Figure 4.5 by substituting a dissatisfaction problem as the *Quality Issue*. The QFD team leader solicits input about how each of the four M categories contributes to the room temperature

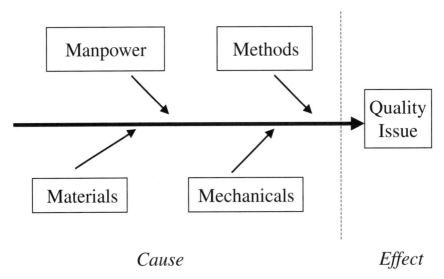

Cause   Effect

FIGURE 4.5.   Cause-and-Effect Diagram Starting Point

problem. As suggestions are offered, they are added to the diagram as branches. The completed cause-and-effect diagram resembles a fish skeleton (Figure 4.6). Because of their appearance, cause-and-effect diagrams are also sometimes referred to as *fishbone diagrams*. Figure 4.6 (also created using Microsoft Power Point™) shows the overall, generic appearance of a cause-and-effect diagram.

Using the four Ms as categories of cause is arbitrary. Depending on the problem and its context, different categories can be used. This is because different problems have different root causes. For example, rather than using the four Ms, the team may decide that using the *four Ps* is more consistent with their problems. The four Ps refer to policies, procedures, personnel, and plant. Whatever causal categories are used, they should be closely related to the problem at hand. Each branch off the main backbone represents a series of possible causes of the focus problem. Branches off each cause represent subcauses of the problem. Taken together, the causes and subcauses should show a pattern

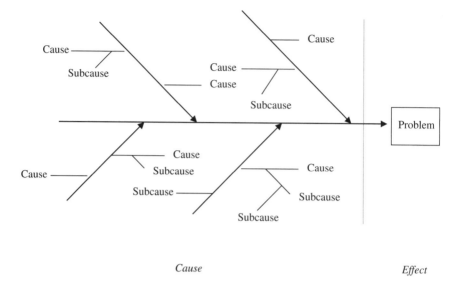

Cause   *Effect*

FIGURE 4.6.   Generic Cause-and-Effect (Fishbone) Diagram

of specific potential sources of the problem at hand that should be investigated and provide clues for possible solutions to the problem itself.

One word of caution about using the cause-and-effect diagram process to solve organizational problems is in order. Management must focus on causal issues they can control. Time spent focusing on issues not under their control is generally wasted. For example, increasing nurse staffing may be a solution to a particular satisfaction-related problem. However, given the current reimbursement climate and the shortage of nurses in some geographic locations, the solution may not be possible to implement. As an alternative, the team should look for solutions they can implement, such as eliminating duplicative services and staffing, eliminating unnecessary services, or finding other staff to perform some of the routine or nonclinical tasks normally performed by the nursing staff. For example, around 45 percent of a nurse's time is spent performing administrative tasks, such as completing forms, charting, and so on.[49] The cause-and-effect diagram should highlight these areas and provide clues for organizational change.

When used properly, the cause-and-effect diagram is an extremely effective tool for solving problems of low patient satisfaction. By deconstructing, or breaking down, the causes of the problem into smaller, more manageable portions, management can develop and implement interventions more efficiently and more effectively.

Scatter Diagrams

Scatter diagrams are used to graphically display the relationship between two variables of interest. A scatter diagram involves mapping the values of two variables on a simple x-y grid. Values of one measure form the x axis of the graph, while values of the other form the y axis. Ishikawa notes that this technique is often used to display a hypothesized cause-and-effect relationship.[46] In this type of application, the cause would be represented on the x axis and the effect would be represented as the y axis. Once the values on the x and y axes have been established, it becomes a simple matter of plotting each case on the graph by the intersecting values on the two axes. Each point on the graph represents a pair of values associated with x and y.

Scatter diagrams provide a graphic view of the direction and strength of the relationship between two variables. Perhaps as important, they can illustrate when a relationship does not exist. For example, suppose we want to examine the relationship between the number of complaints about patient room temperature and daily high temperature over a 60-day period. The results are presented in Figure 4.7 (which was created using Microsoft Excel™ and graphing the spreadsheet entries using the *Scatter Diagram* option).

In this instance, the graph shows a strong positive relationship between the daily high temperature and the number of complaints registered by patients about their room temperature. That is, the general pattern shows that the hotter the outside temperature, the more complaints submitted by patients. This can be determined by the direction of the plotted points on the graph. A plot that appears to flow from the lower left to the upper right portions of

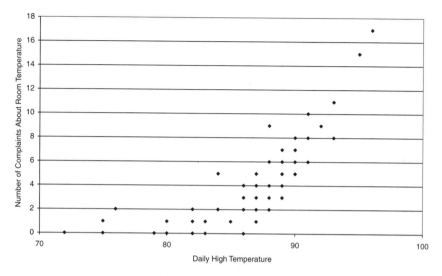

FIGURE 4.7.   Scatter Diagram of Relationship Between Outside
Temperature and Complaints About Room Temperature

the graph represents a positive relationship between the two variables. A movement from the upper left to the lower right portions
of the graph is indicative of a negative relationship. If no pattern
is discernible, it means there is no significant relationship between
the variables. Also, the more dispersed the points on the plot, the
weaker the relationship. Conversely, the tighter the plot, the
stronger the relationship between the two variables. In this example, the relationship between room temperature and outside temperature is strong and positive. In fact, once the outside temperature reaches 90°, the number of complaints tends to rise
considerably. The information these data should provide the management team is that they must be more conscious of room temperature when the weather turns hotter. If they can improve room
temperatures proactively, they should be able to reduce the number of complaints and increase patient satisfaction.

   The scatter diagram could also be used to examine the relationships between departments or areas. For example, scores
relating to physician communication can be correlated with scores
relating to nurse communication to determine the relationship. If

no or little relationship exists between the two, it may demonstrate a need for an intervention designed to coordinate the efforts
of physicians and nurses to provide better and more consistent
information. If there is a strong, positive relationship between the
two, it tells the management team to look elsewhere for solutions.

Control Charts

Control charts are typically used to establish trends in data over
time relative to changes in mean values. Ishikawa provides details
on the calculations and construction methods for control charts
used in production management situations.[46] Often, control charts
are used to evaluate and manage defective products by drawing
samples of the product over time, calculating the mean number of
defects per sample, calculating an upper and lower control limit,
and constructing a graphical representation of the trend over
time. The control chart itself uses time as the baseline (x axis),
and the values of the measured variable appear on the vertical (y)
axis. Three horizontal lines are also included on the graph; the
upper control limit (UCL), the grand mean, and the lower control
limit (LCL). The UCL and the LCL represent values equivalent
to ± three standard deviations around the mean, representing a
probability level of .001.[50,51,52] The mean values are then plotted on
the graph.

The mean number of defects per sample can be examined over
time relative to tolerance limits established by the UCL and the
LCL. If all means fall within the range established by the UCL
and the LCL, the process is deemed *under control.* In theory, any
process must be under control before it can be improved. If mean
values fall either above the UCL or below the LCL, the process is
considered to be *out of control.* Before quality can be improved, the
process must be brought under control. In the production of
machine parts, for example, parts that do not meet engineering
tolerance limits (UCL and LCL) will not properly fit with other
parts, resulting in a defective whole. Clearly, it is imperative that
all parts fit well to ensure a quality product. If the control chart
demonstrates a process under control, management can implement

strategies to improve the process, which will reduce the range of tolerance (the UCL and the LCL).

Using control charts with patient-satisfaction data, however, requires some adjustment in the theoretical orientation of this procedure.[18] For example, although a machined part that exceeds the UCL in size (i.e., it is too large) causes problems for the quality of the finished product, having patient-satisfaction levels higher than the UCL is not necessarily great cause for concern. In other words, we typically are not alarmed by having patients who are *too satisfied* with the healthcare we provide. Scores exceeding the UCL, however, are problematic because they represent a random occurrence rather than something the facility has done to improve satisfaction levels. If the process is random, there is nothing to prevent drastic unexplainable decreases that could exceed the LCL. To manage the overall process, we must get it under control so that it can be improved.

Relevant calculations necessary to construct a control chart are the mean satisfaction score for each sample; the grand mean, or process average, of those scores; the range of scores; the UCL; and the LCL. The sample mean is simply calculated by summing the scores across all respondents from the survey and dividing by the number of respondents in the sample:

$$\overline{X} = \frac{X_1 + X_2 + X_3 \ldots + X_n}{n}$$

where X_n represents individual patient scores and n refers to the size of the sample. The range in scores (R) is calculated by subtracting the minimum score from the maximum score in the sample:

$$R = X_{max} - X_{min}$$

From these calculations, we can establish the process average ($\overline{\overline{X}}$) and the average range ($\overline{R}$) as:

$$\overline{\overline{X}} = \frac{\overline{X}_1 + \overline{X}_2 + \overline{X}_3 + \ldots \overline{X}_n}{k}$$

and

$$\overline{R} = \frac{R_1 + R_2 + R_3 \dots + R_n}{k}$$

where k equals the number of samples.

Using these resulting values, the UCL and LCL are calculated as:

$$UCL_x = \overline{\overline{X}} + A_2 \overline{R}$$

and

$$LCL_x = \overline{\overline{X}} + A_2 \overline{R}$$

In these equations, A_2 represents an adjustment for the number of subgroups in our example. Values for A_2 can be found in Appendix C or in other volumes such as Ishikawa or *The Memory Jogger*[TM].[46,5]

Table 4.2 contains the data derived from patient-satisfaction surveys conducted each quarter over a 5-year period from 1995 through 1999. The values in the table represent the mean composite satisfaction scores (based on a 100-point scale) for satisfaction with ER waiting times. For all the following control chart examples, A_2 is equal to 5, which represents the number of years covering the study. Since data were collected each quarter for a 5-year period, n equals 20 (the equivalent to the number of samples).

Using the results contained in Table 4.2, a control chart can be constructed. (To do so, we have used Microsoft Excel™ to do the calculations and to draw the control chart using the *Line Graph* option. An example of how the spreadsheet was developed is included in Appendix A.) The control chart illustrating patients' satisfaction with ER waiting time is presented in Figure 4.8. This is an illustration of a process that is not under control.

As can be seen from the control chart, the sample means exceed the UCL in four instances and the LCL in four. In other words, 8 of the 20 data points are beyond ± 3 standard deviations of the process average of 88.41. Plus or minus 3 standard deviations

TABLE 4.2. Emergency Room Waiting Time Data

		Month (Quarter)		
Year	Jan.	April	July	Oct.
1995	92.00	88.93	85.23	88.49
1996	89.03	85.29	89.07	88.29
1997	91.97	85.03	87.90	89.86
1998	91.84	89.04	87.10	87.53
1999	87.23	91.84	85.58	86.89
Sum	452.07	440.13	434.88	441.06
n	5	5	5	5
$\overline{X}$	90.41	88.03	86.98	86.89
R	4.77	6.81	3.84	2.97
$\overline{\overline{X}}$	88.41			
$\overline{R}$	4.60			
A_2	.577			

$$\text{UCL}_x = \overline{\overline{X}} + A_2\overline{R}$$
$$= 88.41 + (.577)(4.60)$$
$$= 91.06$$

$$\text{LCL}_x = \overline{\overline{X}} - A_2\overline{R}$$
$$= 88.41 + (.577)(4.60)$$
$$= 85.75$$

represents probability limits of .001.[50,51] In other words, 8 data points are significantly (beyond the .001 level) different from the grand mean. Before we can effectively improve ER waiting times, we must first get the overall process under control. To do so in this case, it would be necessary to examine the individual questionnaire items comprising the composite scores to search for

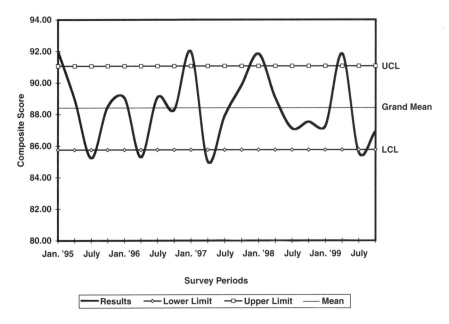

FIGURE 4.8.   Emergency Room Waiting Time Control Chart

clues to the root causes of the problem. This might include examining relevant frequency distributions, histograms, and Pareto charts. Based on these data, intervention strategies can be developed and implemented. Maintaining longitudinal data allows administrators to examine any short- and/or long-term effects of their interventions.

Figure 4.9 illustrates a satisfaction process that is *out of control* in a positive direction. The composite scores for patients' satisfaction with physician care never exceed the LCL but do exceed the UCL in three of the quarters examined. This represents a major difference between production and healthcare applications of control charts. In a production setting, a part that exceeds the UCL is significantly larger than the engineering tolerance permit. That is, the part must be reworked because it will not fit properly with other parts. In healthcare, however, this may not be viewed as problematic. The issue of having patient-satisfaction scores that are too high is a problem most healthcare facilities would like

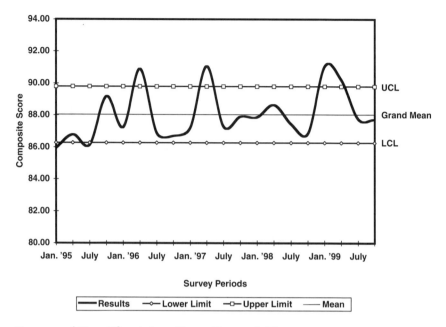

FIGURE 4.9. Physician Care Control Chart

to have. SPC theory, however, dictates that a process must be under control before it can be effectively improved.

The control chart representing composite scores of patients' satisfaction with nursing care is presented in Figure 4.10. In this instance, we have an example of a process that is *in control*. That is, all quarter mean values fall within the boundaries defined by the UCL and the LCL. This illustrates a process that is ripe for improvement. Improving the process means devising intervention strategies to increase the grand mean, the UCL, and the LCL.

The final control chart example, presented in Figure 4.11, illustrates a satisfaction process *under control and improving*. In this case, patients' satisfaction with staff courtesy was under control for at least the first 3 years of these data. Quality improvement efforts resulted in two occurrences. First, the process average increased from 88 to 89. Second, both the UCL and the LCL increased, demonstrating overall improvement. This is an example of the best-case scenario for all organizational processes.

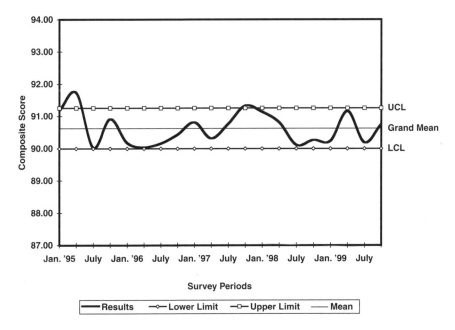

FIGURE 4.10. Nursing Care Control Chart

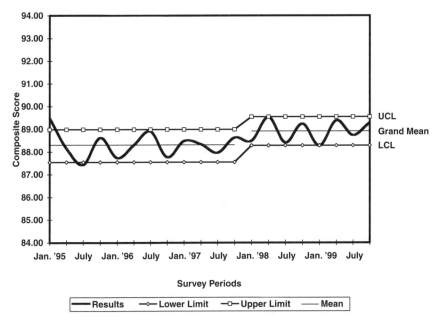

FIGURE 4.11. Other Staff Courtesy Control Chart

Control charts allow managers at all levels of the organization to have a better understanding of what has happened to patient-satisfaction levels over time. Further, they allow management to establish satisfaction targets based on historical performance, as well as providing feedback on the effects of intervention strategies. Target values can be defined based on data for individual items rather than on a uniform increase.

In many cases, upper management decrees that all patient-satisfaction levels must improve by 10 percent across the board. This may be a reasonable request for some areas but not others. For example, let us assume that housekeeping has a score of 70 (on a 100-point scale) while nursing may have satisfaction scores of 90. A 10 percent increase for housekeeping would be 7 points, while a 9-point increase is required for nursing. There are two problems here. First, nursing is, in effect, being punished for doing a good job. They have satisfaction scores 20 points higher than housekeeping, but they are being directed to improve their scores more than a poorer performing area. Second, there is considerable room for improvement for housekeeping (30 points) and very little for nursing (only 10 points). It may be impossible, in fact, for nursing to comply with the directive since it would require nearly perfect scores to do so. Control charts also allow management to determine whether the scores are outside of the expected range of variation as defined by the LCL and the UCL.

Control charts assist managers in setting meaningful and relevant patient-satisfaction objectives. We all agree that patient-satisfaction levels can never be too high. We also realize we cannot please everyone. That is, perfection is an unrealistic target. In the preceding example, a 2-point increase in the mean satisfaction scores for nursing most likely represent a larger impact on the patient-care process than a 7-point increase for housekeeping.

In sum, control charts help management teams focus on the process of patient satisfaction so that it can be understood and improved. Departments with significant performance improvement can be defined as *best-practice* departments, and their successes can be transferred to other areas. Because this is an ongoing measurement process, the effects of interventions are quickly known. Adjustments can be made and measured within a quarter. Most importantly, while the other TQM/CQI tools focus on intervention points, control charts allow the management team to monitor the pulse of patient perceptions of the delivery of medical care.

SUMMARY

Fundamental to the use of TQM/CQI measurement tools is the philosophy that it is better to manage patient satisfaction by data than by myth. Each tool provides a different perspective on the root causes of low patient-satisfaction levels. By focusing on smaller, more manageable aspects of the problem, the probability of implementing successful intervention strategies is enhanced. All of these SPC tools can be incorporated into the patient-satisfaction process with relative ease. Used together, they can provide a clear, detailed picture of the patient-satisfaction process within the institution. Knowing precisely how the patient-satisfaction process works makes improvement more effective and efficient. Analyzing patient-satisfaction data in a systematic fashion on a continuous basis provides invaluable insight into how the organization is viewed by patients. These insights, in turn, allow managers the opportunities to improve the overall performance of their institution. In chapter 6, we provide a case study utilizing the SPC tools discussed in this chapter.

Chapter 5

APPLYING INTERVENTIONS FOR QUALITY IMPROVEMENT

REQUIREMENTS OF ONGOING MEASUREMENTS

To effectively use patient-satisfaction data to improve healthcare quality, the organization must make a long-term commitment to collecting, analyzing, and applying the best data possible to engage in organizational change to improve medical care and service. In any customer-satisfaction program, the healthcare organization is only as good as its last survey. Attention must be paid to every data-collection point. To improve patient-satisfaction levels, management must be prepared to monitor and apply the results on an ongoing basis. Patient satisfaction is a fluid and dynamic process. It is not static, nor is it frozen in time. Rather, the results reflect the process of care in a healthcare organization over the entire survey cycle. Seldom does applying a single intervention result in significant, positive gains in patient-satisfaction levels. More often, multiple interventions are needed to address process issues. For example, the administration may implement a nurse-physician communication program designed to improve nurse knowledge regarding a particular type of patient, while at the same time implementing a new inpatient diagnostic-test-scheduling system to improve process flow. These process solutions may or

81

may not be immediately effective (if at all), or they may achieve desired results at different rates. The only way to be certain that the desired results are being achieved is to measure the effects of the interventions on an ongoing basis.

Ongoing measurement provides the organization with several benefits. First, it allows accurate identification of those process changes that are successful. The name of the game in healthcare today is speed. The turbulence of the healthcare marketplace requires organizations to offer quick responses to the dynamic forces affecting their performance. The faster an organization can improve service and process, the sooner cost efficiencies and quality improvements can be achieved. Cost efficiencies and quality improvements place the organization in a better market position and elevate its financial situation. Monitoring which process changes have resulted in improvement at the departmental level, for example, allows rapid deployment of the success throughout the organization. Learning from success, as well as from failure, improves the learning curve of the organization. That is, the more an organization improves, the more efficient it becomes at improving. Success breeds success. If the institution is part of a multihospital, integrated delivery system, successful process changes can be transported throughout the system for cost and quality gains. In sum, successful interventions can result in improved market position, increased consumer awareness, better financial performance, and negotiation leverage with employers and managed-care companies.

Given this underlying philosophy, the requirements of ongoing measurement are as follows:

- *The survey process must be ongoing.*
  That is, surveys must be conducted on a regular basis (i.e., monthly, bimonthly, or quarterly). Also, the survey must be conducted across the same time interval, using the same data-collection methods, to make the results comparable over time. The consistent and continuous implementation of a solid survey process is key to success.

- *The analysis strategy must be consistent for each survey conducted.*
  The TQM/CQI tools previously discussed are only as good their application. Using the proper measurement tools to evaluate patient-satisfaction levels results in better information and, ultimately, more effective intervention strategies. The combination of speed and success drives the organization's rapid achievement of quality improvement.
- *Points in time where quality interventions are implemented must be marked for identification.*
  Fluctuations in patient satisfaction can be the result of random variation, as well as identifiable causes. Interventions designed for a specific outcome must be planned to remove random variation and create a specific measurable effect. Sometimes, random variation takes care of itself. By definition, a random shift is unexplainable and probably temporary. If no root cause for the problem can be found, it is unlikely that an effective intervention strategy can be developed.
- *The survey instrument must be adaptable, so questions can be added to help measure process improvement and any innovations affecting patients.*
  Patient satisfaction is dynamic. As patients become more sophisticated regarding medical outcomes, their expectations will rise. Early analysis and recognition of the effects of these changes provide cost and quality improvement opportunities. Organizations must be ready and able to quickly take advantage of these situations through intelligent intervention and accurate assessment of the intervention's effect.
- *The peer group selected for benchmark comparison must be monitored for accuracy of comparisons.*
  If, after having made quality improvements, the institution achieves its benchmark standard goal, a new comparison

group will be necessary. Ultimately, an organization's objective should be to achieve breakthrough improvements in relation to an industry, not merely to its defined peer group. That is, an organization should strive to be the industry leader and not be content in the middle of the pack.

- *The survey strategy and process should not be dramatically changed during the course of improvement work.*
  If the data-collection process is outsourced, the organization should not regularly change patient-satisfaction vendors. Of course, there may be situations when it becomes necessary to change vendors. It must be remembered, however, that changing vendors may place the institution in the situation of taking one step forward and two steps back. Vendor changes should be made based on quality and usefulness criteria rather than solely on the basis of cost. If the organization is using an in-house survey instrument, *major* changes in the questionnaire or the sampling frame should be avoided. The problem is that results may not be comparable across instruments and opportunities for improvement may be lost.

- *Successes must be shared throughout the organization.*
  Information must be shared across departments to foster an atmosphere of institutional quality. Any number of techniques—from departmental manager presentations to quality fairs and storyboards—may be used to accomplish this task. The important thing is to reinforce the importance of measurement as an ongoing tool for success in the attitudes and behaviors of all staff. Focusing on really using patient-satisfaction information is of paramount importance.

- *Short- and long-term improvement goals provide the necessary requirement for ongoing measurement.*
  Through analysis of patient-satisfaction data, changes in performance can be identified. The objective should be to

measure the outcome of the change, not the process or activity of the change. Examining the outcomes associated with quality improvement interventions may point toward faulty implementation, however. Be prepared to switch strategies if an intervention is unsuccessful.

- *Be prepared to continuously evaluate the impact of interventions on levels of patient satisfaction.*
  Some interventions succeed; some fail. The key is to identify successes and expand on them throughout the organization and to retool failed interventions to change them to successes.

Any patient-satisfaction program must be ongoing, consistent, and measurable. The analysis of patient-satisfaction data and the measurement of outcomes should demonstrate change over time. Hopefully, the change will be positive, resulting in an improved financial position and elevated patient perceptions of quality. Through ongoing measurement, it is possible for the culture of the organization to be changed. This results in a more responsive customer-friendly environment for patients and employees.

USING RESULTS TO BUILD A CULTURE OF SATISFACTION

What is a *culture of satisfaction?* A culture of satisfaction can be defined as an organizational environment dedicated to the purpose of creating and keeping customers through the mechanism of satisfaction. Organizations with a culture of satisfaction design products and services based on the needs and input of their customers. The performance in the area of customer satisfaction from the chairman of the board to the line staff in the organization is not only focused on providing benchmark customer service performance but also continually redefines the industry in the way customer satisfaction is delivered. The culture of satisfaction is not a fashionable program, nor is it merely a slogan. It is an environment where one of the key organizational values is a focus on people. The culture of satisfaction includes written employee performance appraisals, and the standard of customer service behavior is reviewed on a regular basis. A culture of satisfaction involves developing and maintaining written position qualifications that measure and demand specific behaviors indicative of customer-focused employees. The culture thrives on rigorous performance measurement, not necessarily against a peer group, but always against itself to improve performance. The organization's mission, vision, and values reflect the importance of a satisfied customer and are disseminated throughout the institution. The organization commits money and other resources to provide training programs and continually strives to update the customer-relation skills of its employees. Patient perceptions of satisfaction are closely monitored, and the time, energy, and resources to make meaningful change are part of a major organizational commitment. Finally, the organization committed to a culture of satisfaction does not talk in financial terms but in human relation terms. They understand that financial success comes directly from improving patient satisfaction, not the other way around.

The first step in building a culture of satisfaction is to use data appropriately. The old adage that *you cannot get somewhere unless you know where you are going* is very true here. Displaying data in charts and graphs, along with using other measurement tools, can add a sense of focus and detail to areas requiring improvement. Patient feedback is the single most powerful force an institution has to provide direction and to foster change. Ignoring patient feedback will result in lower levels of satisfaction and reduced utilization rates.

The second step is for senior management to utilize these data to create the atmosphere for change through active participation and management in the patient-satisfaction process. A fundamental requirement of TQM as espoused by Deming is the complete dedication and involvement of upper management.[40] This may call for a realignment with the board of directors of the mission, vision, and values of the organization. It will require senior management to immerse themselves in the culture of satisfaction. It will also require the institution's leadership to measure their own

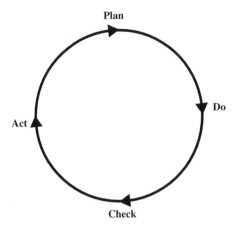

FIGURE 5.1. The Plan, Do, Check, Act (PDCA) Cycle

performance relative to areas of patient satisfaction selected for improvement. It requires leadership and decision making based on facts and not on myth. It is, in short, leadership by example.

Finally, the third part of the process in building a culture of satisfaction is to instill a sense of organizational involvement. This comes from analyzing the patient-satisfaction data at the departmental level. Through the *plan, do, check, act (PDCA) cycle,* also known as the Shewhart cycle,[40] employees become empowered to develop innovative solutions to process problems, resulting in a change in the culture of the organization. The PDCA cycle (Figure 5.1) begins by focusing on the problem at hand, developing a team of key employees to work on solving the problem, and establishing a *plan* of attack. The *do* phase of the cycle follows by measuring the extent of the problem and implementing a strategy for improvement. Once the intervention has been implemented, its effects must be accurately measured during the *check* part of the cycle. Finally, the effects of the intervention must be evaluated to determine its level of success or failure in solving the original problem. Based on the evaluation, the team returns to the *plan* phase of the cycle and repeats the process.

Yet, these steps would not be complete without intensive customer service training. Customer service excellence is an ongoing process based on the needs of the employees and the customers. One cannot assume that customer service without training will automatically come about. Not all individuals would be on the same level, so varying levels of the program would be needed. Based on assessments of the individuals skill level to provide acceptable levels of customer service, programs could be designed in a sequential order to address fundamental issues. Such programs already exist and are available. Going outside of the healthcare industry to Home Depot, Ritz Carlton, Hyatt, or Marriott will give you a new perspective and approaches without reinventing the wheel.

The organization's focus on internal process to reduce costs and improve quality must change to one that employs the voice of the customer to drive cost and quality improvement initiatives. Change occurs when individuals become accountable to the reactions and perceptions of patients to the internal processes of the hospital. An organization that is using patient-satisfaction data in a voice-of-the-customer program will be forced to create a culture of satisfaction. No organization can continue to operate the way it has done in the past in the face of a continuous data stream indicating negative customer perceptions of its service delivery. Change becomes a continuous force in the drive to create a satisfied customer. Without satisfied customers, success is unattainable.

METHODS TO ENSURE MANAGERIAL BUY-IN

The most difficult, yet most effective, method to ensure managerial buy-in is to incorporate the results of the patient-satisfaction survey into the performance appraisal system. Each performance appraisal system should have an employee-specific objective or set of objectives related to improving patient-satisfaction ratings. This includes all employees in the organization—from the president of the hospital, who is responsible for the overall quality rat-

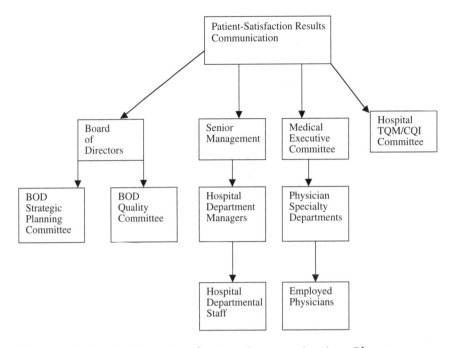

FIGURE 5.2. Patient-Satisfaction Communication Chart

ings, to the managers and employees of specific departments. Performance increase can be tied to the quality ratings that patients give any provider. For example, a percentage of a year-end incentive compensation could be tied to fluctuations in patient-satisfaction ratings for the department that would fall within ± 2 percent of the standard baseline score. Figure 5.2 illustrates how results could be deployed throughout the organization on a regular and formal basis.

Another strategy might be to make quarterly, gain-sharing payments to all employees based on meeting or exceeding the organizational target for the aggregate medical outcome score. This type of performance appraisal may be acceptable within the private inurement provisions of the Medicare regulations and is used by several major health systems that the authors are aware of. As with all potential interpretations of incentive payments and safe harbor regulations, legal counsel should be consulted. Gain-sharing payments or incentive payments to employees should be based on quality indicators rather than on financial performance. This is a critical point. As tax-exempt entities, hospitals and health systems cannot use excess revenues after expenses for private gain. Private gain would result if performance incentive compensation was based purely on the financial performance of the organization. By tying performance incentives to quality gains, the financial arguments seem to be removed.

Quarterly reports to the board strategic planning committee, quality committee, general board of directors, medical executive committee, physician department meetings, and at department manager meetings are effective ways to communicate and report the facility's progress toward patient-satisfaction targets. At the board level, an effective patient-satisfaction status briefing would focus on aggregate scores and trends in the major areas of the measurement system, areas targeted for improvement, and improvement goals for the following quarter. Too much information or too detailed information could lead the board to micromanage the organization, which could, in turn, interfere with staff efforts to accomplish organizational goals. The purpose of the patient-satisfaction briefing is to give the board members an overview of how their customers perceive the institution and what progress is being made toward improvement. The following discussion illustrates how this may look.

In creating a culture of satisfaction, voice-of-the-customer programs and voice-of-the-process programs will, at some point, require additional resources to implement. In a time of increasingly scarce resources, boards are more likely to approve major expenditures to improve quality and customer satisfaction if they have been involved from the beginning. As stated previously, building a culture of satisfaction requires the commitment of the entire organization. Including the *board of directors* in this process sends a strong and powerful signal to the entire organization that everyone is dedicated to quality improvement.

Physicians are the toughest audience you will face in this process. Since physicians control about 80 percent of the resource consumption in your organization, it is imperative to involve them in this process. Historically, physicians have been quite autonomous and independent in terms of practice, behavior, and accountability.[36] In addition, because of the nature of the patient-practitioner relationship, physicians routinely hear from their patients about what works and what does not within the institution. Engaging in a constructive dialogue centered around the voice-of-the-customer process helps build a culture of satisfaction and helps draw the physicians into the process. Additionally, meeting with the physicians on a regular basis to review patient-satisfaction survey data presents an opportunity to provide constructive feedback on how patients perceive the care they provide. This is an aspect of the care process they might not be totally familiar with, because patients are often reluctant to confront physicians directly with complaints about the way the physician provided care. When results are presented as group data rather than as individual data, physicians are more likely to participate in the process of satisfaction. The goal is to make physicians active participants in the improvement process, not to make them defensive about their caregiving skills. Usually, physician-related scales from patient-satisfaction survey data are the most consistent over time, with little variation from the previous quarters. There are clues in the data on how physicians communicate and interact with their patients in the inpatient setting. Improvements in the various aspects of the patient-practitioner relationship go a long way toward improving patient perceptions of the quality of care provided by the entire institution.

Often, the most important activities for senior management center around the strategic plan, its successful implementation, and the reporting of major accomplishments to the board of directors. Yet little time is typically spent in the planning process detailing targets for improving customer satisfaction. An argument can be made that patient-satisfaction improvements are actually areas of daily management. However, they are also strategic in nature because they affect the profitability, market position, and the brand image of the institution.

Most strategic plans cover five major areas: *medical staff integration, ambulatory care/primary care development, operations improvement, integrated delivery system development,* and *managed care/capitation.* We maintain that *patient satisfaction* should be included as a sixth area. Including an objective related to patient satisfaction elevates the stature of organizational efforts to create a culture of satisfaction.

In this case, specific outcomes to be achieved annually over a 3-to-5-year strategic planning period might include increasing patient ratings of overall medical care by a targeted percentage. A 3-to-5-year objective would be to institute a patient-employee communication program that sets certain percentage increase benchmarks to be achieved. An overarching goal would be to become the benchmark hospital in its class for patient satisfaction and positive impact the industry. The result is to send the message that customer satisfaction is a high priority of the organization. It also sends the message that high levels of customer satisfaction are important to the long-term survival of the hospital and are treated as such. This, in turn, forces quarterly reporting to the board of directors and assists in the process of clarifying expectations and results.

Financial reporting and correlation are critically important, as well. Trends in financial measures, such as hospital earnings, net revenue per bed, and return on assets, need to be correlated with overall patient-satisfaction scores.[4] There should be a strong positive correlation between the two measures. That is, as patient-satisfaction levels increase, profitability goes up. As patient-satisfaction levels go down, profitability declines. Areas that need to be monitored closely for financial impact include medical and billing systems and the discharge process.[4] Additionally, the Finance department should conduct cost-benefit analyses of quality initiatives using an approach such as the Taguchi method calculation of the *quality loss function (QLF).*[53] In this calculation, the dollar cost of quality improvement can be estimated. The QLF demonstrates what happens to the price of quality based on financial criteria. It is useful in deciding which course of action has the highest possible return for the dollar spent. The calculation of the QLF takes the following form:

$$L = kv^2$$

where

$$k = A/\Delta^2$$

and represents the costs associated with rework and v^2 is the mean squared deviation from the target value. Δ represents the tolerable variation in the product.

Let us walk through a numerically simple example of a healthcare application of the QLF. Suppose a hospital is reimbursed $3000 for a particular diagnosis related group (DRG), which has an approved length of stay of 3 days. The average length of stay (ALOS) for this DRG at this facility is 2.5 days with average costs of $1000 per day. Overall, therefore, the hospital is making an average of $500 per day on each case with the focal DRG. By examining variance reports and reviewing the analysis of readmissions, the administration has concluded that the probability of a readmission greatly increases if the ALOS is reduced below 2.25 days. On the other hand, if the ALOS goes above 3 days, costs are greater than the reimbursement, which results in a monetary loss. Therefore, it was determined that an acceptable mean deviation from the ALOS of 2.5 days is .25. That is, if the length of stay can be maintained between 2.25 and 2.75 days, losses due to readmissions from early discharges and over-stays will be at a minimum. The current average deviation from the ALOS is one day. The administrative team has decided to develop and apply an intervention designed to reduce this variation in this DRG's ALOS by 50 percent.

The amount of money lost to poor quality can be estimated by the QLF for both scenarios. The costs saved by the intervention can be estimated by subtracting the loss attributable to each level of deviation from the ALOS. The data necessary to do so follow:

$$m = \text{ALOS} = 2.5$$
$$A = \text{Readmission ALOS} = 2.5$$
$$V = \text{Average deviation from } m = 1.00$$
$$\Delta = \text{Acceptable deviation from } m = .25$$

Applying these data to the QLF,

$$K = A / \Delta^2$$
$$= 2.5 / .25^2$$
$$= 2.5 / .0625$$
$$= .15625$$

and

$$L = KV^2$$
$$= (.15625)(1.00)^2$$
$$= .15625$$

Therefore, the cost of quality lost in the current situation is roughly .15 days per patient within the DRG. If we can reduce the variation in ALOS from one day to half a day, we can calculate the reduction in loss per patient due to the improvement. The value of K remains the same, but the value of V becomes .5. The value for L is calculated as

$$L = KV^2$$
$$= (15625)(.5)^2$$
$$= (.15625)(.25)$$
$$= .03906$$

The values associated with L represent the per patient loss due to low quality in days. Each value of L can be multiplied by the costs per day for the DRG to arrive at a monetary value. Since the cost to the hospital for this DRG is $1000 per day, the current process results in a loss of $156.25 per patient. If the variation in ALOS could be cut in half, the loss per patient would be reduced

TABLE 5.1.   Quality Improvement by Tightening Treatment
             Deviation

	Tolerance	V	K	V²	Expected Quality in Days	Expected Dollar Loss/Patient
Current	m ± .25	1.00	.15625	1.00	.15625	$156.25
Tightened	m ± .25	.50	.15625	.25	.03906	$ 39.06
Value of Improvement						*$117.19*

to $39.06 per patient. Table 5.1 summarizes the results from this
hypothetical example and shows that quality improvement could
result in a savings of $117.19 per patient. Multiplying this value
by the total number of patients in the DRG category results in an
estimate of the total increase in revenue due to the intervention.

FROM STRATEGIC INTERVENTION TO THE STRATEGIC PLAN

Because continuous organizational dedication to improving
patient satisfaction is necessary, it must become part of the
organization's strategic plan. The long-term solutions to patient-
satisfaction problems require that interventions be an integral
part of the institution's strategic vision. However, as Batalden[54]
warns, such commitment must be integrated with organizational
policy and cannot be viewed as only required written statements
in the strategic plan. Doing so, of course, requires the support,
leadership, commitment, and absolute dedication of the institution's upper management team to transforming the entire
organization.

Tindill and Stewart provide the following "winning management strategies for organizational transformation:

1. The organization acknowledges that customers are the
   most important part of the healthcare system. They are

both a beneficiary and a part of the TQ process.
Customer requirements, or needs, determine both the
desired outcome of the process and how it should work.

2. Management makes a long-term commitment to
   integrate the continuous improvement process of TQ
   into the management structure (through such elements
   as strategy, planning, and leadership—modeling desired
   actions and attitudes, etc.).

3. Reward systems reinforce new behaviors required in the
   TQ system. The organization appropriately recognizes
   both managers and employees for their successes and
   contributions.

4. All organization members focus on opportunities for
   improvement, convinced that these represent
   opportunities for future success.

5. Everyone contributes to the continuous improvement
   effort because they know that preventing problems is
   better than reacting to them.

6. Management empowers and supports all members of the
   organization so they can fully participate in the TQ
   system with teams and as individuals. They place great
   value on both personal and mutual, team-based
   development, recognizing that human capital is the most
   important asset of the organization.

7. Everyone recognizes that problems are usually the result
   of system failures rather than human failures. Instead,
   they analyze and resolve problems in the context of an
   overall process. Thus, the focus is on improving the
   process, not blaming people within it" (pp. 218–19).[55]

These principles of a successful total quality (TQ) program implementation also directly apply to the development of a patient-
satisfaction program. Success is predicated on dedication from
the top to the bottom of the organization chart.

SUMMARY

Organizational change requires managerial change and buy-in. By combining information with accountability and action, organizations can achieve levels of patient satisfaction, that not only become a benchmark but also redefine performance in relation to an industry. Without training and communication, these changes cannot be sustained, hence the importance of extensive and ongoing customer service training. Examples abound in other service industries on how to create an organizational culture and system to create that high-performing culture. Modifying the program that best suits your organization can increase the speed of change required, achieving better performance. Finally, the financial cost of not providing quality customer service can and should be an analysis that is fundamental to the survival of the organization.

Chapter 6

A CASE STUDY

BACKGROUND

For purposes of this text, we have created a fictitious hospital to serve as a contextual example. Kentwood Memorial Hospital (KMH) is a full-service facility located in an urban environment with a population of approximately four million. It is not a member of a developing multihospital, integrated delivery system, having made a conscious strategic decision to remain autonomous. With a large central city core and surrounding suburbs, KMH serves a patient population of 500,000 while competing with four other acute-care hospitals. There is little market differentiation among the hospitals as the public views them as essentially the same in terms of services delivered and the quality of care provided. KMH is a *level 2 trauma center*, licensed for 350 beds, although it is currently staffing only 150 beds. KMH owns an attached medical office building, housing between 50 and 75 physicians. Although some tenants are multispecialty groups, most are solo practitioners. All physician tenants are high admitters to KMH. In addition, the hospital owns several primary-care physician practices in highly attractive suburban locations.

Some of KMH's key annual statistics are:

- 12,000 admissions
- 100,000 outpatient visits
- 50,000 ER visits
- 1200 births
- An average length of stay of 4.0 days
- An average daily census of 146

KMH is technologically up-to-date with the latest MRI, CT, digital cardiac catheterization laboratory, and state-of-the-art operating rooms. Key service lines for KMH include Orthopedics, Women's Health, Geriatric Medicine, Diagnostic Cardiology, Oncology, and Neurology.

In a stage 2 managed-care environment, around 30 percent of KMH's revenues are derived from managed-care contracts, with another 48 percent coming from Medicare. The KMH physician-hospital organization (PHO) is engaged in some limited capitation arrangements covering around 5000 patients with 250 physician members. The hospital is fully accredited by the Joint Commission on Accreditation of Health-care Organizations (JCAHO) and is tax-exempt under the Federal Tax Code.

THE KMH PATIENT-SATISFACTION PROCESS

KMH has developed an extensive patient-satisfaction mail survey program. Each quarter, KMH surveys inpatient and ER patients using an outside patient-satisfaction organization. Areas commonly surveyed include:

- Medical outcomes
- Nursing care
- Physician care
- Food service
- Housekeeping
- Admitting/discharge
- Support services
- Other staff courtesy

A series of questions is asked under each of these categories. Additionally, two other questions are asked of all respondents. The first question is, *Would you return to this facility for medical care?* The second question is, *Would you recommend this facility to others?* Questions across categories are aggregated to form scales that probe and measure patient-satisfaction levels for key areas of service delivery and care environment.

Rather than drawing samples each quarter, KMH conducts a census, surveying every patient who has used the facility during the previous 3 months. Surveys are conducted in January, April, July, and October each year. Response rates generally hover around 50 percent. Quarterly results are shared with department managers, the board of directors, and the medical executive committee, and are presented at physician departmental meetings.

The KMH management team has incorporated patient-satisfaction data into its organizational strategy to improve the quality of care they provide. Senior executives and department managers have goals and objectives related to increasing patient-satisfaction scores above national peer-group norms as part of their incentive compensation program. The leadership of KMH routinely uses the six tools to help implement their TQM/CQI philosophy regarding patient satisfaction. A major part of this philosophy is to manage and improve the patient-satisfaction process using data rather than relying on "gut" instinct or myth. Based on the data analyses, departmental targets for improvement are calculated and assigned. Through these analyses, department managers determine areas of impact requiring intervention. All results are monitored on an ongoing basis. Departmental experiences (positive and negative) are shared hospital-wide to improve the evaluation and intervention process.

PLAN

Each quarter, the Kentwood QFD team meets to review and discuss the most recent results of their patient-satisfaction survey. During these meetings, data are examined to determine where

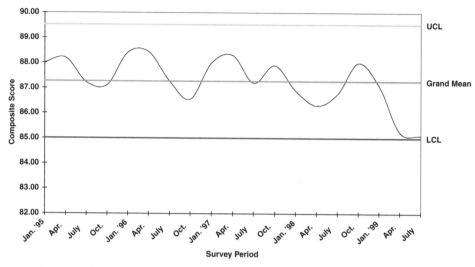

FIGURE 6.1.   Nurse Communication Control Chart

problem areas might exist. During the regular meeting in April 1999, the QFD team noticed a rather sharp decline in the *nurse communication scale* scores. Realizing that there had been some turnover in the nurse staff, the team decided to wait another quarter before taking any action. One quarter's score does not necessarily represent a trend. That is, the dip may have been random in nature rather than the beginning of a downward trend in the data. The decision was made to wait another quarter to see if the trend self-corrected.

When the July data were received, the QFD team began by focusing on the nurse communication scale scores. An examination of the control chart for this measure indicated a continuation of the low scores (Figure 6.1). Although the scores are still within the boundaries of the LCL, a continued trend would drive the process out of control. A unanimous decision was made to engage in a detailed investigation of the source of the problem and to develop an intervention strategy aimed at alleviating the problem.

To conduct the evaluation of the nurse communication problem, the QFD team decided to draw other key hospital personnel

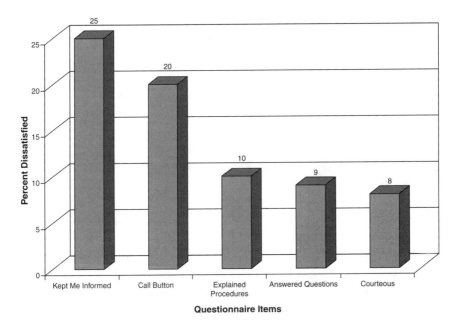

FIGURE 6.2.   Pareto Chart of Nurse Communication Items

into the process. In addition to QFD team members, several nurses, physicians, administrators, and ancillary staff personnel were brought together with an initial directive of establishing the root causes of the decline in the scores. Together, the group formed the *nurse communication improvement (NCI)* committee.

DO

During the initial meeting, the NCI committee began focusing on the problem at hand. Their first step was to begin narrowing the parameters of the problem by examining the individual items comprising the nurse communication scale. It was necessary to determine whether patients were dissatisfied with all aspects of their interactions with the nursing staff or whether particular items were driving the composite scores downward. To do so, the committee reviewed a Pareto chart of the scale items (Figure 6.2).

The Pareto chart compares the percentage of patients reporting being either *Somewhat Dissatisfied* or *Very Dissatisfied* with the item. The five questionnaire items examined are responses to the following:

How satisfied were you with
How courteous the nurses were?
How well the nurses kept me informed about my case?
How quickly the nurses responded to the call button?
How well the nurses explained medical procedures?
How well the nurses answered my questions?

The figure indicates that the levels of dissatisfaction with the nursing staff's communication center around two items: keeping patients informed and responding to the call button. Based on these data, the NCI committee agreed their focus would be on improvement in these two areas.

Several committee members raised the issue on physician communication as well. Their concern was, in effect, that if the nursing staff is not communicating well with patients, perhaps the physicians are not doing as well as they should. Although no major problems in the *physician communication scale* score were found, and improving physician communication was not part of their charge, the NCI committee realized that there is likely a strong correlation between the two scales. As a result, the committee decided to examine a scatter diagram displaying the relationship between the nurse communication scale and the physician communication scale (Figure 6.3).

The scatter diagram showed a strong positive relationship between the two composite scores. This was illustrated by the direction and the tight clustering of the points on the graph. Based on the data displayed in the scatter diagram, the NCI committee concluded that if they could improve nurse communication, there would very likely be a *spillover* effect on physician communication. That is, if the nurse communication scores could be significantly improved, the physician communication scores should also show improvement.

The next step taken by the NCI team was to focus on the two individual items located on the Pareto chart. Table 6.1 contains the

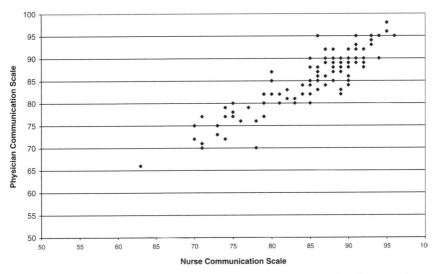

FIGURE 6.3.   Scatter Diagram of Nurse Communication Scale
and Physician Communication Scale

TABLE 6.1.   Distribution of responses to *How satisfied were you
with how well the nurses kept you informed?*

Response Category	Percent
Very Satisfied	50
Somewhat Satisfied	25
Somewhat Dissatisfied	15
Very Dissatisfied	10
Total	100

frequency distribution for the question relating to keeping the
patient informed. The frequency distribution indicates that not
only is the level of dissatisfaction high at 25 percent, but the percentage of patients who are very satisfied is quite low (50 percent).

A similar pattern was found in the frequency distribution of
responses to the question relating to how quickly the nursing staff

TABLE 6.2. Distribution of responses to *How satisfied were you with how quickly the nurses responded to the call button?*

Response Category	Percent
Very Satisfied	42
Somewhat Satisfied	38
Somewhat Dissatisfied	11
Very Dissatisfied	9
Total	100

responded to the call button. The distribution of these data is contained in Table 6.2. In fact, although the percentage of dissatisfied patients is lower, so is the percentage of patients who were very satisfied with the nurses' response to the call button (42 percent).

Based on the data, the NCI committee decided to brainstorm to arrive at some conclusions concerning the causes of the problem. While brainstorming, the committee engaged in building a fishbone diagram. They began with a generic template such as the one displayed in Figure 4.5 and divided the diagram into four quadrants representing the four Ms (materials, mechanicals, methods, and manpower). Possible causes of poor nurse communication were discussed and added as branches and subbranches off the main backbone of the diagram. Using the four Ms to analyze potential causes of low levels of satisfaction with nurse communication allowed the NCI committee to focus on different areas of the process in a structured way.

The NCI committee began with *materials* in their discussion of root causes of the satisfaction problem. The committee concluded that nurses possibly spend too much of their time stocking supplies in their departments. This, in turn, results in less time being spent with patients. It follows that nurses communicate less with patients. Similarly, the committee determined that if supplies run low, nurses will spend an inordinately greater amount of their time searching for the supplies they need. This reduces the amount of time spent with patients and lowers the amount of communication nurses have with patients. The fishbone diagram developed by the Kentwood NCI committee is shown in Figure 6.4.

Moving to *mechanicals,* the NCI committee determined that inefficiencies in the hospital's information system may result in information relating to patients' cases not being provided in a timely manner. As a result, nurses have less information to give patients, which lowers their level of communication with patients. It was also noted that the units themselves may be poorly designed, resulting in wasted efforts by the staff. This would result in less time spent with patients and lower communication levels.

An examination of the *methods* portion of the process showed that problems admitting patients to the units result in nurses wasting time dealing with inappropriate admissions. This, in turn, results in less time spent with patients and less communication with patients.

Manpower issues clearly relate to understaffing. A staff shortage results in nurses caring for a larger number of patients than they would in fully staffed units. This, of course, means they spend less time with each patient. Less communication follows from reduced time spent with individual patients.

Examined as a whole, the fishbone diagram points to several possible causes of the low levels of patient satisfaction with nurse communication. The NCI committee concluded that the root causes could be grouped into the following categories:

Nurses do not spend enough time interacting with patients.

KMH's information system needs upgrading to improve the timeliness and quality of the information provided to nurses.

Units should be redesigned to make nurses' jobs more efficient.

The admissions department must develop strategies to decrease the number of inappropriate admissions.

Additional RNs must be hired to alleviate the staffing shortages.

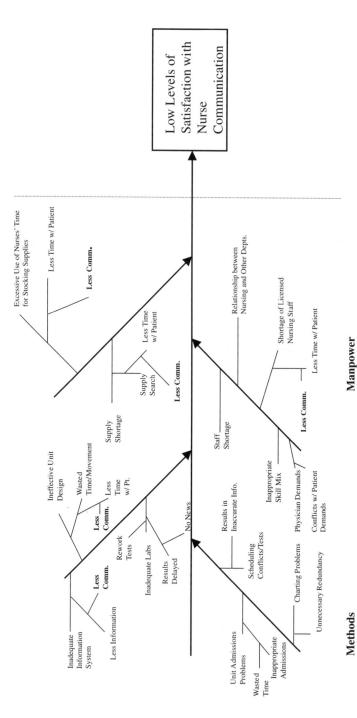

Mechanicals

Materials

Inadequate Information System

Less Information

Ineffective Unit Design

Wasted Time/Movement

Less Comm.

Less Time w/ Pt.

Supply Shortage

Rework Tests

Inadequate Labs

Results Delayed

No News

Results in Inaccurate Info.

Scheduling Conflicts/Tests

Charting Problems

Unnecessary Redundancy

Unit Admissions Problems

Wasted Time

Inappropriate Admissions

Excessive Use of Nurses' Time for Stocking Supplies

Less Time w/ Patient

Less Comm.

Supply Search

Less Time w/ Patient

Less Comm.

Staff Shortage

Relationship between Nursing and Other Depts.

Shortage of Licensed Nursing Staff

Less Time w/ Patient

Less Comm.

Inappropriate Skill Mix

Physician Demands

Conflicts w/ Patient Demands

Low Levels of Satisfaction with Nurse Communication

Methods

Manpower

FIGURE 6.4.   Fishbone Diagram Applied to the Problem of Low Levels of Nurse Communication

108

After a brief discussion, the NCI committee concluded that effecting major changes in KMH's information system (IS) and redesigning units were beyond the beyond the purview of the committee. The decision was made to forward concerns and recommendations to the IS committee and the planning committee as input into their strategic planning processes. Further, the NCI committee concluded that any intervention strategies must focus on all of the remaining three areas.

INTERVENTION STRATEGY

The first phase of the intervention strategy focused on freeing time for the nursing staff. This part of the intervention had several components. First, staff from materials management took over responsibility for stocking incoming supplies and closely monitoring stock levels. The objective was to virtually eliminate all nurse concerns about unit supplies. It was hoped that nurses would only have to be concerned when emergency supply shortages occurred. In the event of such emergencies, nurses were to inform the materials management staff of the problem and it would become their responsibility to immediately locate the required supplies.

Second, the admissions process was modified to include a redundancy in checking the appropriateness of every admission. By double-checking each admission, it was hypothesized that the number of inappropriate admissions could be greatly reduced. This would eventually result in giving nurses more time to spend with patients.

Third, the search process for additional RNs was enhanced. A nurse shortage in KMH's community had slowed the hiring process substantially. Additional advertisements were placed in local newspapers. In addition, advertisements were placed in newspapers in neighboring cities, a bonus program was instituted to entice recruits to come to KMH, and ads were added to local radio and television programming.

Fourth, an in-house program was developed and implemented that was designed to reinforce the importance of communicating with patients and to inform the nursing staff of the other intervention components. The focus of this program was on improving nurse communication skills through active participation in skill-building exercises and open discussions related to improving response time to patients using the call button.

The objective of the NCI committee's intervention strategies, taken together, was to allow the nursing staff to spend more time with patients and to improve their communication skills. Ultimately, it was the committee's belief that improvements in these areas would result in improved patient care and greater levels of patient satisfaction.

CHECK

Throughout the process, members of the NCI committee monitored the implementation of their interventions. By the close monitoring of the process, minor problems that were encountered were corrected immediately. For example, as materials management staff began their new duties stocking supplies in the units, it was discovered that the process for emergency stocking of supplies was not working effectively. The original process involved having the nurse requiring supplies complete a request form and deposit it in a box located at the nursing station. On a frequent and regular basis, one of the materials management staff would check the box for orders and immediately respond to any requests. It became clear very quickly that even frequent trips to the nursing station for emergency request forms delayed the process to the extent that the nurses found it faster to locate the required supplies themselves.

The process was modified by making one materials management staff person responsible for emergency supply situations. That staff person was given a beeper so that he could be notified immediately of any problem. After being beeped, he was required to call the nursing station for instructions within minutes. This enhancement completely eliminated the need for nurses to locate supplies on their own. Minor problems in other areas of the intervention were similarly fine-tuned to improve their effectiveness.

TABLE 6.3. Distribution of responses — after intervention — to
*How satisfied were you with how well the nurses kept you
informed?*

Response Category	Percent
Very Satisfied	59
Somewhat Satisfied	23
Somewhat Dissatisfied	11
Very Dissatisfied	7
Total	100

When the following quarter's patient-satisfaction data were received, the NCI committee began a review of the effects of their intervention strategy. The committee began by taking another look at the frequency distributions for the two key focal questions. Table 6.3 contains the frequency distribution for the question related to keeping patients informed about their cases. The results indicate an improvement in both areas of concern. First, the percentage of patients dissatisfied with how well they were kept informed was reduced from 25 percent to 18 percent. Second, the percentage who were *Very Satisfied* with this item increased from 50 percent to 59 percent.

More dramatic improvements were found in satisfaction levels with response time to the call button. The frequency distribution for this item after the intervention is located in Table 6.4. In this case, the level of overall dissatisfaction decreased from 20 percent to 11 percent. Dramatic decreases were found in the *Very Dissatisfied* category, where the percentage dropped to only 2 percent. In addition, the percentage of respondents answering *Very Satisfied* increased from 42 percent to 62 percent, an improvement of 20 points.

The post-intervention Pareto chart (Figure 6.5) of the items comprising the nurse communication scores showed some interesting shifts. First, levels of dissatisfaction for all five items

TABLE 6.4.　Distribution of responses — after intervention — to *How satisfied were you with how quickly the nurses responded to the call button?*

Response Category	Percent
Very Satisfied	62
Somewhat Satisfied	27
Somewhat Dissatisfied	9
Very Dissatisfied	2
Total	100

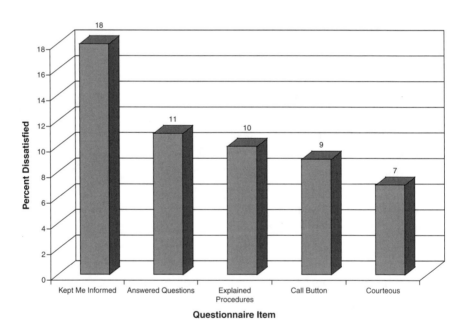

FIGURE 6.5.　Post-intervention Pareto Chart of Nurse Communication Items

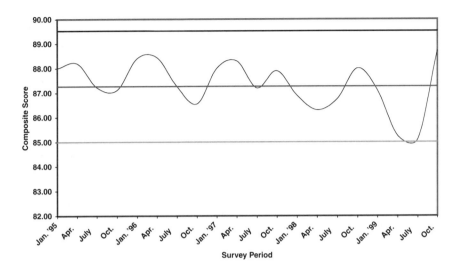

FIGURE 6.6.   Post-intervention Nurse Communication Control Chart

decreased. Second, the item related to response time to the call button went from being the second most important item to the fourth most important. Finally, although the percentage of patients reporting dissatisfaction with how well they were kept inform decreased, it remained the most important item.

Next, the NCI committee reviewed the control chart for the nurse communication scores for improvements. The post-intervention control chart (Figure 6.6) shows that the October 1999 data showed a sharp improvement. The upward turn in the nurse communication scores provided some evidence that the committee's intervention strategies were meeting KMH's objectives.

ACT

The results presented are indicative of short-term success. Of course, KMH is interested in long-term improvements. In the *act* phase of the PDCA cycle, the NCI committee concluded that they were on the right track in terms of elevated levels of nurse communication within the organization. The recruitment process met with limited success. Although new nurses were hired, some existing nurses left KMH. The net effect was a minor reduction in the nursing staff shortage. It was decided to extend the recruitment strategy that was already in place and begin the development of a retention program.

The NCI committee concluded that, although nurses' time had been substantially reallocated to patient care and there were substantial improvements in response time to the call button, greater improvement was necessary in other areas. The committee decided to continue the PDCA cycle by returning to the *plan* stage. It was decided that the in-house program focusing on the importance of keeping patients informed should be continued and expanded to include role-playing exercises designed to improve the nurses' communication skills and to give nurses practice and direction on how to answer questions and explain procedures to patients in clear, nontechnical terms. The effects of these enhancements will be measured and reviewed for effectiveness.

SUMMARY

By using the PDCA cycle and SPC tools, it was possible for KMH to effectively improve patient satisfaction with nurse communication. The continuous measurement of patient-satisfaction items and review of intervention strategies should result in long-term gains for the hospital. Measuring the nurse communication scores the following quarter and adding them to the control chart will provide clues as to whether the improvements seen in October were random or the beginning of an improved process.

Chapter 7

CONCLUSION

The journey to focus your hospital or health system on using patient-satisfaction data to improve quality begins with the realization of the importance of listening to the voice of the customer. Our approach emphasizes using statistical-process-control tools and techniques to gain greater insight into the process of satisfaction in your institution. Understanding how patient-satisfaction levels affect the organization's overall performance provides tremendous opportunity to develop and implement improvement strategies. As we have already argued, to take advantage of this opportunity requires a strong leader. The institution needs an executive-level "champion" who is willing to take up the challenge to educate, to inform, and to drive home the importance of patient satisfaction to maximizing the organization's mission and to improving performance. To get the job done will require changes in behavior and attitude in a way that is uncommon in healthcare today. It requires creating a culture that benefits patients, that provides quality and cost improvements, provides opportunities yet undiscovered, improves the bottom line, and, finally, teaches every employee how to listen to and attempt to truly understand the institution's customers.

What has been suggested here is not a magic bullet, nor is it a quick fix. It represents a long-term investment in the future of the organization. The expected return of this investment is an improved financial position, improved market position, and highly satisfied patients. The issue of how to begin the organizational transition necessary to realize such benefits must be addressed. We have alluded to the fact that change must be supported from the top of the organization's administration and must be embraced and implemented throughout the institution. What follows is practical advice on how to follow through.

STARTING AT THE TOP

Nothing changes in an organization unless the chief executive officer (CEO) has sent out a clear message of vision and direction to the institution. The CEO must be the visionary that can drive this process, obtain the board of directors' approval and commitment, and communicate to the organization through words, deeds, and actions the importance of an organizational focus on patient satisfaction. But this change does not simply go through asking the CEO to pronounce the new program. It requires the CEO to become actively involved. Although it may be perceived as dangerous to engage in a dramatic shift to a new organizational focus, it is necessary. We believe the CEO should lead at least one patient-satisfaction-data-driven quality improvement team. We believe that the CEO should also be the chief quality officer of the hospital or health system. It has been our general observation that those organizations with the highest quality and lowest cost have the CEO leading the battle charge, setting the tone, and keeping the vision on track. Visible and active leadership from the CEO broadcasts the clear and strong message that patient satisfaction is the organization's top priority. Improving patient satisfaction will help generate organizational success. As Deming said, "What you need are customers who are more than happy. You need customers who boast about your product. That return-repeat customers. There's the gravy. Your fixed costs are all paid" (p. 30).[40]

Many may argue that the CEO should not be involved in the day-to-day operations of the facility. This is true in many ways, but how many CEOs in today's marketplace are not involved on a daily basis? We propose a strategy based on 30-day plans. The changes we propose through the use of these techniques leave no room for the fainthearted or slow to act. Using patient-satisfaction data to improve organizational performance requires swift problem analysis, solution identification, and intervention implementation. For example, if the patient-satisfaction surveys are conducted every 3 months, there is essentially a 30-day window of opportunity to analyze, develop, and implement a potential solution. During the remaining 60 days preceding the next round of surveys, interventions can be implemented. Then, when the following quarter's survey is completed, the institution will have some valid and reliable data on the impact of the changes made. If it appears that the intervention is not being successful, fine-tuning can be completed quickly to get back on track. Therefore, for all intent and purposes, the CEO is actually only leading one team for 30 days. The CEO does have to do the work, but his/her presence reinforces the organizational commitment to the process and outcomes. Further, once the data-analysis systems are set up, basic analyses require inputting current data.

The next most important figure in the transformation may be the chief financial officer (CFO). Left out most of the time, the CFO and his or her staff need to be brought into the equation. There should be a member of the accounting staff assigned to each QFD team to calculate the financial impact of not making a quality improvement. Additionally, the finance individual needs to determine what the net impact to the bottom line will be. In many places, quality improvements and cost reductions are not always monitored and accounted for. There needs to be a mechanism that clearly illustrates the net effects and bottom-line improvements from improvement programs. In sum, bring in the finance people as part of the teams and hold them accountable for some aspect of the program. Show the entire organization that improving patient satisfaction is not just a feel-good exercise, but that it controls 17 percent to 27 percent of the variation in hospital profitability.[56] We believe the CFO should lead the QFD team for all billing process and other financial issues.

The chief operating officer (COO), as with the CEO and CFO, needs to become actively involved in the start-up of this process as well. Dealing mostly with day-to-day operating issues, the COO is the logical choice to lead those efforts related to physical plant operations, housekeeping, and so on. Though there may be quality teams for projects in place, it is necessary to bring in the housekeeping and maintenance individuals for the comfort and cleanliness portion of the satisfaction improvement process. Creating an organization-wide culture of satisfaction requires the active involvement of all the senior executives in the organization. Having the triangle of the CEO, CFO, and COO actively working with patient-satisfaction data will provide them with another perspective of how patients view their world.

Other senior managers such as the vice president of patient services, the chief nursing officer, the vice president of administration, and various other vice presidents of clinical service lines have already been involved in one way or another with CQI programs. They should already have a base understanding of the process. What is new is the concept of using patient-satisfaction data to drive clinical quality improvements. Resistance results from the misconception in the industry that patients are unable to judge the technical quality of the healthcare they receive. Research has shown and continues to verify the fact that patients do have the knowledge and understanding to make technical judgments of quality. These judgments are, more often than not, in sync with the technical views of hospital quality as held by the physicians.[12] It is imperative to invoke a paradigm shift in the attitudes of clinical service line senior managers to gain a better understanding of the nature and usefulness of patient-satisfaction data. This attitude shift is made possible through the active, visible involvement of upper management.

BRINGING ALONG THE MIDDLE MANAGERS

Another program, another way to make us do more work, another fad, is how many of the middle managers will react. *We already have quality teams, we look at data, and we have made significant changes to the organization. Why do we have to do this one now? What is so different about this program? When do we have the time, energy, or training to analyze, create, and implement quality improvement plans in 30 days?*

The simple answer is *You have no choice.* In the days, weeks, and months ahead, opportunities for change will be limited, the competition will grow more complex and increasingly intense, and patients will become more demanding than before. Along with firm, upper-management commitment, education is key to success. The unknown and the unexplainable are frightening to many. To look critically at what your patients are really attempting to communicate is a new experience. A shift in emphasis from what the institution's *clinical experts* have to say to listening closely to what *patients* have to say about their care is major. Staff do not like to believe that patients think their healthcare is anything less than excellent. A critical examination of patient-satisfaction data can mobilize and reenergize an organization to achieve new levels of quality and cost improvements.

This type of program is a competitive weapon in a high-stakes game of organizational survival. As we have tried to demonstrate, patient views of quality are key to that survival. Patients reflect their views through patient-satisfaction surveys. The financial impact of increasing quality by at least one standard deviation increases your margin 2 percent. Additionally, a satisfied patient is more likely to be a loyal patient who will return for care and will recommend your hospital to others. Opportunities for access-managed-care contracts and better rates will open as employers attempt to meet their employees' demands for better service. Patient satisfaction is a competitive weapon, largely ignored by the industry, but one that influences every hospital and health system manager on a daily basis. So, what can be done to succeed in implementing a patient-satisfaction program?

First, it is imperative to educate and train the managers on the importance of patient satisfaction. Although this sounds simple, many middle managers do not have a sound understanding of how patients make decisions regarding the selection of healthcare providers, how they view their healthcare experience, or what they, as consumers of a service, expect from the facility. Knowledge is power, and managers must be empowered through education.

Second, working with the CEO, CFO, or COO on a patient-satisfaction QFD team brings home the realization of the importance of the project. As stated earlier, nothing convinces an organization more than when the top leadership is involved. It is imperative to go beyond merely expounding on an organizational vision by committing to and becoming actively involved in the implementation of the vision. Working with the CEO and CFO gives these individuals the opportunity to experience, firsthand, the talent available within the organization. Managers have the opportunity to perform, achieve success, and position themselves for advancement within the organization. Continuing their educational process helps to maintain continuous organizational improvement.

Third, high-performing departments that provide exceptional customer service as reflected by the data should become showcase departments. It is important to learn and to share experiences in this process because it is easier to replicate success than to recreate it. At the monthly managers' meeting, department managers can present case studies on how they achieved high performance. Lessons shared across the organization are lessons learned by the organization. Even small successes should be celebrated. Managers of high-performing departments can help encourage other department managers to improve their departmental performance. No one likes to be seen as different from his or her peer group. Like physicians, department managers already know who is good and who does not perform up to their potential. A little internal competition can bring about positive organizational change. Professional papers focusing on successful intervention strategies can be presented at professional meetings and published in professional journals.

The fourth place to make an impact and motivate individuals is in the area of compensation. Adding goals and objectives with measurable and tight performance criteria that are linked to patient-satisfaction scores and attaching a dollar value to those performance measures further stress the importance of the program. For example, an objective may be to have the aggregate patient-satisfaction score for a department be within plus or minus two standard deviations of a target score to receive a *meets the objective* rating. To receive an *exceeds objective* rating, the aggregate score must be within one standard deviation around the aggregate department score. Anything below the target score does not meet the improvement target and negatively impacts the manager's performance appraisal and incentive compensation. The intent is not to be punitive, but to drive meaningful change.

Finally, now is the time to bring in the marketing and marketing communications people. It is critically important to communicate information on the progress of the patient-satisfaction improvement program in a concise, informative, and regular way. Information on what patients think, how the institution is improving, and what that improvement means to the organization as a whole needs to be disseminated across the organization and the community. The goal should be to create a high-performance hospital and health system that is based not only on the financial factors of success but upon the views of your patients. Marketing becomes the glue of the effort to create a true culture of satisfaction. Efforts of the organization should be communicated and celebrated both internally and externally, as well.

The marketing strategy employed should reflect the organization's commitment to improving levels of patient satisfaction. A marketing communications strategy to the broader public should include this topic also. The goal is to gain market position. If an institution can set itself apart from the competition by being the market leader, everyone else becomes an *also ran*. The competitive hospitals and health systems will be forced to play *catch-up*. The important point is that announcing patient-focused accomplishments will increase the distance between you and your competition.

Physicians will want to be associated with you, patients will want to come to you, and employers will demand that you be included in managed-care plans because their employees recognize the excellence of your facility.

EMPOWERING LINE STAFF

For this type of quality improvement to be successful, line staff must be actively involved. Though often preached and seldom followed, line staff — the housekeepers, registration clerks, maintenance personnel, dietary aides, and transportation aides — are most often left out of quality improvement programs. Organizational change on a massive scale requires no less than the full and complete participation of all employees. Managers must understand that healthcare organizations are not democracies, nor are they plantations, and that employees are a critical element of any quality improvement effort. The day-to-day staff are the ones who come in constant contact with patients. The program described in this book relies very heavily on these individuals. It will be necessary for them to carry out the program, to feed back the informal organization's assessment of patient perceptions, and to make patient-satisfaction improvement efforts a reality. The line staff understands how the system works and, through their direct contact with the patients, they understand the patients' true view of the organization.

Every department must be involved in a quality program that is driven by patient-satisfaction data. Patients see the hospital as an interrelated collection of departments working together for their benefit. Line staff must take the same view in order to resolve operational delays and system process problems and to get a very complicated process of care to work efficiently and effectively. Armed with this body of knowledge, line staff will be able to make the improvement program a success. All staff need to be included in the celebration of gains brought about by the program. All things considered, they will create the culture of satisfaction that leads to a high-performing, patient-focused, data-driven organization. Education, training, universal involvement, and senior management support to do the right thing will empower individuals to take responsibility for the success of the program. Bringing in line staff to accomplish the objectives of the organization is empowering them to act in the best interests of patients and the organization. Everyone in the organization has something positive to offer, and their inclusion will increase the probability that the institution's overall performance will be elevated.

INCLUDING PHYSICIANS

Always your toughest critics and constantly hearing from their patients about their positive and negative experiences, physicians play an important role in the success of a patient-satisfaction program. They are a valuable source of additional information that can supplement your efforts. Also, they can and must address areas of general patient perceptions of physician care. Though their satisfaction scores may already be high, we could expect that, as other areas such as nursing care perceptions improve, there would be a corollary improvement with physicians as well. After nurses, physicians are the most important link in the patient-satisfaction chain.

Because of their severe time constraints, physicians will not be able to serve on many committees or attend many meetings, but they can provide an assessment of improvement actions to be implemented. The nonvocal physicians who understand the nature of satisfaction, have high-performing practices themselves, and can add significant insight into your operational quest should be viewed as a major resource. The question, of course, is *Will they participate?* The answer to that question will depend on any number of internal hospital or system issues. It will depend on whether the physicians view your organization as one committed to creating a partnership for the benefit of the patient. In using patient-satisfaction data to drive quality and cost improvements, everybody wins.

This is never quite as simple as it sounds because the dynamics of the politics and the relationships with hospital leadership, past (usually failed) efforts to shape medical staff behavior, and the physician's own perceptions and attitudes come into play and may pose barriers to participation. Perhaps relations between senior staff and the physicians are strained. In this case, it may not be possible to involve the medical staff in the beginning. However, this should not deter the efforts to create a culture firmly based in the principle of customer satisfaction. As your efforts take shape and satisfaction scores improve, physicians will eventually participate. Many of these same techniques can be used in large multi-specialty group practices, small groups, groups without walls, and solo practices. If physicians can be convinced they have a vested interest in improving levels of patient satisfaction, they will eventually become active and willing participants in the program. Many of the mechanisms that patients use to determine levels of hospital satisfaction are also at play in the physician's office. If their own financial bottom line improves as a result, even greater enthusiasm will develop. In short, bringing the physicians into the overall process will further enhance even an already successful intervention.

MAKING MARKETING RESPONSIBLE

We would like to offer one final suggestion as you move forward. As with all things, many individuals within organizations have vested interests in a variety of outcomes. We suggest that marketing, if they are already not responsible, be made accountable for managing the patient-satisfaction surveys and the patient-satisfaction improvement process. If anyone in the organization understands customer satisfaction and its impact, it is marketing. They have education, background, experience, and the resources necessary to educate, inform, and communicate to the hospital or health system the program. They have the marketing communications skills to develop and disseminate the message internally and externally. They have the market research resources to establish the data-analysis systems and monitor the survey results on an ongoing basis. Using marketing is one way to focus the organization on the prize of higher levels of patient satisfaction, improved quality, and improved financial importance. Often, by acting as a third party, marketing can serve as an arbitrator in efforts to focus departments on the root causes of patient dissatisfaction, through the use of unbiased data analysis. They can, in effect, let the numbers speak for themselves.

INTEGRATED DELIVERY SYSTEMS
AND MANAGED-CARE APPLICATIONS

Throughout this text, we have focused on the hospital-based applications for several reasons. First, hospitals have been engaged in the formal measurement of patient satisfaction longer than other healthcare entities. With this wealth of experience and available data, the implementation of the techniques described here should be relatively easy to incorporate into existing strategies. Hospitals should, therefore, be positioned to take a leadership role within the industry. Second, hospitals remain the most costly component of the U.S. healthcare delivery system. They are also the major revenue generation component. The potential financial efficiencies to be gained through improvement in patient-satisfaction levels are greatest at the hospital level. Third, consumers tend to identify with the local hospital rather than with the system that owns the hospital.

The techniques described in this text can be simply expanded across an integrated delivery system (IDS) to help improve the performance of other members and of the system as a whole. Local hospital successes can be deployed across the system. Although the IDS may be viewed as an integrated set of services, the best place to measure and control quality is at the point of service. Similarly, the best place to measure and improve patient-satisfaction levels is at the level where care is provided.

Smaller entities can apply the techniques as well. Ambulatory care facilities can use the techniques to improve quality by improving satisfaction levels. When applied to managed-care organizations (MCO), the results of the careful examination of patient-satisfaction data can result in functional improvements and can illuminate opportunities for improvement. Data collected on enrollee-satisfaction levels can allow MCOs to compare different systems, individual hospitals, physicians, or other components to find the best performers. The best performers can be used as benchmarks of quality standards that can be applied across contractual arrangements. The application of the tools and techniques presented here by MCOs should result in higher retention rates and a higher quality network.

THE FUTURE OF PATIENT SATISFACTION

The measurement of patient satisfaction has grown in importance and in sophistication for healthcare organizations. Its importance will continue to grow as reimbursement rates decline or level off and healthcare organizations strive to compete for a shrinking patient base. Healthcare consumers are demanding higher levels of service for their money and will become increasingly willing to change their source of care to what they perceive as a higher quality provider. Patients make those decisions of quality based on how satisfied they are with the care they receive.

Methods of data collection are also likely to see major changes. The use of in-room, computer-assisted, bedside systems; waiting room kiosks; television touch-screen systems, and other point-of-care measurement strategies are likely to increase in the near future. This will allow organizations the opportunity to maintain instantaneous and continuous data collection that will provide feedback on patient perceptions of service quality. Healthcare administrators must be able to invoke rapid and meaningful change in response to shifting patient perceptions. By incorporating data-analysis strategies into the process, administrators will be better equipped to improve quality quickly and maintain a higher level of organizational success.

SUMMARY

This text started with the idea that patient-satisfaction survey data contain a wealth of information upon which to make quality and cost improvements in the hospital. This concept has not yet been widely adopted in the healthcare industry. To achieve new levels of patient or customer satisfaction, one must be ready to challenge and become the change agent of an organization. One must be ready to become the champion and leader. Satisfaction is not just a program, a slogan, or a topic of discussion. It is a way of life that permeates the organization and spurs individuals within to achieve ever-higher levels of performance.

To get the job done, everyone from the CEO down to the lowest position on the organization chart must commit to improving patient-satisfaction levels. Upper management must lead, middle management must supervise and monitor, and all employees must dedicate themselves to implementing the strategy. Only an integrated effort can bring about long-term, continuous improvements in the organization's overall performance.

Appendix A

LIST OF PATIENT-SATISFACTION
MEASUREMENT COMPANIES

The authors wish to make it clear that we do not favor or recommend any particular product, service, program, or company specializing in patient-satisfaction measurement. This list is provided as a service to our readers should they wish to pursue the use of a third party in their patient-satisfaction programs. Additionally, this is not intended to be an exhaustive list of patient-satisfaction measurement companies. To the best of our knowledge, the information presented is correct.

Dey Systems, Inc.
230 Executive Park
Louisville, KY 40207
502-896-8434
www.dey-systems.com

The Gallup Organization
North American Operations
301 South 68th Street Place
Lincoln, NE 68510
402-489-9000
www.gallup.com

**Professional Research
Consultants**
11326 "P" Street
Omaha, NE 68137
800-428-7455
www.prconline.com

National Research Corporation
Gold's Galleria
1033 O Street
Lincoln, NE 68508
402-475-2525
www.nationalresearch.com

129

Parkside Associates
205 W. Toughy Avenue,
Suite 204
Park Ridge, IL
847-698-9866
www.parksideassociates.com

Press, Ganey Associates, Inc.
404 Columbia Place
South Bend, IN 46601
800-232-8032
www.pressganey.com

The Picker Institute
1295 Boyleston Street,
Suite 100
Boston, MA
617-667-2388
www.picker.org

The Jackson Group
Box 1662
Hickory, NC 28603
828-328-8968
www.thejacksongroup.com

Sigma Group
5960 Vandervoot Drive,
Ste. 110
Lincoln, NE 68516
402-420-7979

For managed care and employers:

**National Committee for
Quality Assurance (NCQA)**
HEDIS Users Group
2000 L Street, NW, Suite 500
Washington, DC 20036
202-955-3500
www.ncqa.org

Appendix B

STATISTICAL-PROCESS-CONTROL-ANALYSIS-TOOLS CONSTRUCTION EXAMPLES

HISTOGRAM

Figure B.1 illustrates the use of Microsoft Excel™ to create a histogram. The example shown here is the spreadsheet used to create Figure 4.3. To develop the graph, follow these instructions:

1. Click on the *Graph Wizard*.
2. Click *Next*.
3. Select *Column* chart and choose desired style from the selections offered.
4. Click *Next*.
5. Highlight *Data Range* (cells D6 through D9).
6. Select *Series In Columns* option.
7. Click *Series* tab.
8. Click *Category (x) Axis Labels* bar and click and drag the *x*-series labels from the spreadsheet (cells A6 through A9).
9. Add titles and axis labels information.
10. Click *Next*.
11. Save graph as a chart or insert it into the spreadsheet.
12. Click *Finish*.

	A	B	C	D	E	F	G
1							
2							
3							
4	Component			%		f	F
5							
6	Very Satisfied			32.4		190	190
7	Somewhat Satisfied			50.7		298	488
8	Somewhat Dissatisfied			10.0		59	546
9	Very Dissatisfied			6.9		41	587
10							
11				100.0		587	

FIGURE B.1.   Histogram Example. Satisfaction with Most Recent Visit.

PARETO CHART

The spreadsheet used to construct the Pareto chart represented by Figure 4.4 is contained in Figure B.2. The spreadsheet is comprised of only two columns of information. Column A contains the satisfaction category labels and Column E contains the percentage of respondents rating room environment items as fair or poor. The Pareto chart is constructed as follows:

1. Click on the *Graph Wizard*.
2. Click *Next*.
3. Select *Column* chart and choose desired style from the selections offered.
4. Click *Next*.
5. Highlight *Data Range* (cells D6 through D9).
6. Select *Series In Columns* option.
7. Click *Series* tab.
8. Click *Category (x) Axis Labels* bar and click and drag the *x-series* labels from the spreadsheet (cells A6 through A9).
9. Add titles and axis labels information.
10. Click *Next*.
11. Save graph as a chart or insert it into the spreadsheet.
12. Click *Finish*.

	A	B	C	D	E	F	G	H
1								
2								
3								
4								
5								
6								
7								
8					% Fair/			
9	Item				Poor Rating			
10								
11	Room Temperature				19			
12	Room Cleanliness				7			
13	Housekeeping Courtesy				4			
14	Overall Opinion of Housekeeping				3			
15	Hospital Cleanliness				2			

FIGURE **B.2.**   Pareto Chart Example. Percentage of Respondents Reporting Fair/Poor Ratings

SCATTER DIAGRAM

Figure B.3 contains the spreadsheet used to create the scatter diagram located in Figure 4.7. This particular spreadsheet contains only two columns of data. The first column (Column A) contains the number of complaints about patients' room temperature over a 60-day period. Column D contains the associated daily high outside temperatures for the same 60-day period.

To construct the scatter diagram:

1. Click on *Chart Wizard*.
2. Select the *XY (Scatter)* option.
3. Click *Next*.
4. Select the *Data Range* by clicking on the first data entry (cell A7) and dragging the pointer to the last data entry (cell A66). This will be the data series represented on the y (or vertical) axis on the graph.
5. Click the *Series* tab.
6. Click the *X Values* box.

	A	B	C	D	E
1					
2					
3					
4	# Complaints about			Daily High	
5	Room Temperature			Temperature	
6					
7	0			75	
8	0			72	
9	0			72	
10	1			75	
11	0			75	
12	2			76	
13	6			88	
14	5			84	
15	7			89	
16	9			92	
17	7			90	
18	2			82	
19	1			82	
20	0			82	
21	1			83	
22	0			83	
23	6			90	
24	5			89	
25	1			80	
26	3			86	
27	4			86	
28	4			88	
29	0			80	
30	0			79	
31	2			88	
32	1			87	
33	1			85	
34	1			85	
35	2			86	
36	3			87	

FIGURE B.3.   Scattergram Example *(Continued)*

	A	B	C	D	E
37	1			83	
38	6			90	
39	8			90	
40	5			90	
41	3			88	
42	2			84	
43	0			86	
44	3			88	
45	8			91	
46	6			91	
47	2			88	
48	4			87	
49	6			89	
50	3			89	
51	3			89	
52	5			90	
53	3			88	
54	2			87	
55	8			93	
56	8			93	
57	9			92	
58	9			90	
59	5			89	
60	9			88	
61	5			87	
62	10			91	
63	9			92	
64	17			96	
65	15			95	
66	11			93	

FIGURE B.3.   *Continued*

7. Move to the first data entry of the second series (cell D7). Depress and hold the *Control* key, click and drag to the end of the series (cell D66). At this point, the basic scatter diagram should be seen.

8. Click *Next*.
9. Add any appropriate titles.
10. Click *Next*.
11. Save as a *Sheet*.
12. Click *Finish*.
13. Note that *Excel*™ automatically sets the scale used for the x and y axes. To adjust the scales to individual needs, click on the axis to be adjusted to highlight.
14. Select *Format* from the main bar.
15. Select *Selected Axis*.
16. From the *Format Axis* window, select the *Scale* tab.
17. Change the values of the scale as necessary. In Figure 4.7, the minimum was adjusted to 70 and the maximum was adjusted to 100.

CONTROL CHARTS

The control charts in chapter 4 were developed using the *Microsoft Excel*™ line graph option. Figure B.4 contains the spreadsheet used to create Figure 4.8. Five columns of information are required to construct the control chart. The first column (A) contains the labels representing the data-collection time points. These reflect the 24 quarters of survey data. Column B contains the mean composite satisfaction scores for the *emergency room waiting time* items. Column C contains the lower control limit (LCL) for these data. The LCL was calculated in cell H20 and copied to cells C6 through C25. The formulas used in all the calculations presented in this example are presented in Figure B.5. Next, Column D contains the upper control limit (UCL) data calculated in cell H21 and copied. Finally, Column E contains the process average or grand mean for the entire data-collection period. This value was calculated in cell H16 and copied down Column E.

The steps necessary to construct the control chart follow:

1. Click on the *Chart Wizard*.
2. Select the *Line Graph* option. Please note that we use the *Smooth Line* option selected under the *Custom Types* tab for aesthetic purposes. Any of the *Line Graph* options will work.

3. Click *Next.*
4. Select the *Data Ranges* by clicking on the first data-entry cell (cell B6) of the first series (mean) and dragging to the last data-entry value (cell B25).
5. Move the pointer to the first data-entry element of the second series (LCL cell C6). Hold the *Control* key down while clicking and dragging to the last entry of the series (cell C25).
6. Repeat Step 5 for the third data series (UCL) in cells D6 through D25.
7. Repeat Step 5 for the fourth data series (*Process Average*) in cells E6 through E25.
8. Click the *Series* tab.
9. Click the *Category (x) Axis Labels.*
10. Click and drag the quarter labels from cells A6 through A25.
11. Change each *Series* label to the identifiers in the graph's legend (e.g., Mean, LCL, UCL, Grand Mean).
12. Click *Next.*
13. Add appropriate titles to the control chart.
14. Click *Next.*
15. Save as a chart.
16. Click *Finish.*

	A	B	C	D	E	F	G	H	I	J	K	L
1												
2												
3												
4					Process							
5		Mean	LCL	UCL	Average			January	April	July	October	
6	Jan. 95	92.00	85.75	91.06	88.41		1995	92.00	88.93	85.23	88.49	
7	Apr.	88.93	85.75	91.06	88.41		1996	89.03	85.29	89.07	88.29	
8	July	85.23	85.75	91.06	88.41		1997	91.97	85.03	87.90	89.96	
9	Oct.	88.49	85.75	91.06	88.41		1998	91.84	89.04	87.10	87.53	
10	Jan. 96	89.03	85.75	91.06	88.41		1999	87.23	91.84	85.58	86.89	
11	Apr.	85.29	85.75	91.06	88.41							
12	July	89.07	85.75	91.06	88.41		Total	452.07	440.13	434.88	441.06	
13	Oct.	88.29	85.75	91.06	88.41		N	5	5	5	5	
14	Jan. 97	91.97	85.75	91.06	88.41		$\bar{X}$	90.414	88.026	86.976	88.212	
15	Apr.	85.03	85.75	91.06	88.41		R	4.77	6.81	3.84	2.97	
16	July	87.90	85.75	91.06	88.41		$\bar{\bar{X}}$	88.41				
17	Oct.	89.96	85.75	91.06	88.41		$\bar{R}$	4.60				
18	Jan. 98	91.84	85.75	91.06	88.41							
19	Apr.	89.04	85.75	91.06	88.41		UCLX	91.06				
20	July	87.10	85.75	91.06	88.41		LCLX	85.75				
21	Oct.	87.53	85.75	91.06	88.41							
22	Jan. 99	87.23	85.75	91.06	88.41							
23	Apr.	91.84	85.75	91.06	88.41							
24	July	85.58	85.75	91.06	88.41							
25	Oct.	86.89	85.75	91.06	88.41							

FIGURE B.4. Emergency Room Waiting Time Composite Scores

	A	B	C	D	E	F
1						
2						
3						
4					Process	
5		Mean	LCL	UCL	Average	
6	34700	92	=H20	=H19	=H16	
7	Apr.	88.93	=C6	=D6	=E6	
8	July	85.23	=C7	=D7	=E7	
9	Oct.	88.49	=C8	=D8	=E8	
10	35065	89.03	=C9	=D9	=E9	
11	Apr.	85.29	=C10	=D10	=E10	
12	July	89.07	=C11	=D11	=E11	
13	Oct.	88.29	=C12	=D12	=E12	
14	35431	91.97	=C13	=D13	=E13	
15	Apr.	85.03	=C14	=D14	=E14	
16	July	87.9	=C15	=D15	=E15	
17	Oct.	89.86	=C16	=D16	=E16	
18	35796	91.84	=C17	=D17	=E17	
19	Apr.	89.04	=C18	=D18	=E18	
20	July	87.1	=C19	=D19	=E19	
21	Oct.	87.53	=C20	=D20	=E20	
22	36161	87.23	=C21	=D21	=E21	
23	Apr.	91.84	=C22	=D22	=E22	
24	July	85.58	=C23	=D23	=E23	
25	Oct.	86.89	=C24	=D24	=E24	

FIGURE B.5. Emergency Room Waiting Time Composite Scores *(Continued)*

	G	H	I	J	K
1					
2					
3					
4					
5		January	April	July	October
6	1995	=B6	=B7	=B8	=B9
7	1996	=B10	=B11	=B12	=B13
8	1997	=B14	=B15	=B16	=B17
9	1998	=B18	=B19	=B20	=B21
10	1999	=B22	=B23	=B24	=B25
11					
12	Total	=Sum(H6:H11)	=Sum(I6:I11)	=Sum(J6:J11)	=Sum(K6:K11)
13	N	5	5	5	5
14	$\bar{X}$	=H12/H13	=I12/I13	=J12/J13	=K12/K13
15	R	=H6-H10	=I10-I18	=J7-J6	=K8-K10
16	$\bar{\bar{X}}$	=(H14+I14+J14+K14)			
17	$\bar{R}$	=(H15+I15+J15+K15)			
18					
19	UCLX	=H16+(0.577)*(H17)			
20	LCLX	=H16-(0.577)*(H17)			
21					
22					
23					
24					
25					

FIGURE B.5. *Continued*

140

Appendix C

COEFFICIENTS FOR CALCULATING A_2 VALUES USED IN CONSTRUCTING CONTROL CHARTS

TABLE C.1.   Table of Factors for $\overline{X}$ Charts.

Number of Observations in Subgroup (n)	Factors for $\overline{X}$ Chart A_2
2	1.880
3	1.023
4	0.729
5	0.577
6	0.483
7	0.419
8	0.373
9	0.184
10	0.308

Reprinted with permission from GOAL/QPC, *The Memory Jogger*™ (2 Manor Parkway, Salem N.H., 1988).

References

1. Weingarten, S. 1999. "Assessing and improving quality of care." pp. 467–510 in *Introduction to Health Services,* ed. S. J. Williams and P. R. Torrens. Albany, N.Y.: Delmar.

2. Fitzpatrick, M. J. 1994. "Performance improvement through quality improvement teamwork." *Journal of Nursing Administration* 24(12): 20–27.

3. Davis, S. L., and M. A. Greenly. 1994. "Integrating patient satisfaction with a quality improvement program." *Journal of Nursing Administration* 24(12): 28–31.

4. Nelson, E., R. Rust, A. Zahorik, R. Rose, P. B. Batalden, and B. Siemanski. 1992. "Do patient perceptions of quality relate to hospital financial performance?" *Journal of Health Care Marketing* 12(4): 6–13.

5. GOAL/QPC. 1988. *The Memory Jogger™: A Pocket Guide of Tools for Continuous Improvement.* Methuen, Mass.: GOAL/QPC.

6. GOAL/QPC Research Committee. 1995. *The Voice of the Customer.* Methuen, Mass.: GOAL/QPC.

7. Krowinski, W. J., and S. R. Steiber. 1996. *Measuring and Managing Patient Satisfaction.* Chicago: American Hospital Association.

8. Aday, L. A., R. Andersen, and G. V. Fleming. 1980. *Health Care in the U.S.: Equitable For Whom?* Beverly Hills: Sage.

9. DiMatteo, M. R., and D. D. DiNicola. 1982. *Achieving Patient Compliance: The Psychology of the Medical Practitioner's Role.* New York: Pergamon Press.

10. Rhee, S., R., Bell, T. F. Lyons, and B. C. Payne. 1991. "Determinants of compliance among hypertension patients: Toward an explanatory model." *OHSR Research and Education Series* 1 (2).

11. Wolinsky, F. D. 1996. *The Sociology of Health: Principles, Professions, and Issues.* Belmont, Calif.: Wadsworth.

12. Nelson, E. C., R. D. Hays, C. Larson, and P. B. Batalden. 1989. "The patient judgment system: Reliability and validity." *Quality Review Bulletin* 15(6): 185–91.

13. Lane, P., and J. D. Lindquist. 1988. "Hospital choice: A summary of the key empirical and hypothetical findings of the 1980s." *Journal of Health-Care Marketing* 8(4): 5–20.

14. Ware, J. E., and A. R. Davies. 1983. "Behavioral consequences of customer dissatisfaction with medical care." *Evaluation and Program Planning* 6(4): 291–97.

15. Shimshank, D. G., M. C. DeFuria, J. J. DiGiorgio, and J. Getson. 1988. "Controlling disenrollment in health maintenance organizations." *Health-Care Management Review* 13(1): 47–55.

16. Marquis, M. S., R. D. Davies, and J. E. Ware. 1983. "Patient satisfaction and change in medical care provider: A longitudinal study." *Medical Care* 21(8): 821–29.

17. Woodside, A., L. Frey, and R. Daly. 1989. "Linking service quality, customer satisfaction, and behavioral intention." *Journal of Health Care Marketing* 9(4): 5–17.

18. Bell, R., M. J. Krivich, and M. S. Boyd. 1997. "Charting patient satisfaction: Tracking the effects of patient satisfaction with control charts will add value to your business strategy." *Marketing Health Services* (summer): 22–29.

19. Brown, S., and T. A. Swartz. 1989. "A gap analysis of professional service quality." *Journal of Marketing* 53(2): 92–98.

20. Kravitz, R. L., J. E. Rolph, and K. McGuisan. 1991. "Malpractice claims data as a quality improvement tool: Epidemiology of error in four specialties." *Journal of the American Medical Association* 266(15): 2087–92.

21. Haug, M., and B. Lavin. 1983. *Consumerism in Medicine: Challenging Physician Authority.* Beverly Hills: Sage.

22. Parsons, T. 1951. *The Social System.* New York: Free Press.

23. Ryan, M. J., and W. P. Thompson. 1997. *CQI and the Renovation of an American Health-Care System: A Culture Under Construction.* Milwaukee: ASQ Quality Press.

24. Rundall, T. G., D. B. Starkweather, and B. R. Norrish. 1998. *After Restructuring: Empowerment Strategies at Work in America's Hospitals.* San Francisco: Jossey-Bass.

25. Rubin, H. R., M. S. Gandek, W. H. Rogers, M. Kosinski, A. McHorney, and J. E. Ware. 1993, "Patients' ratings of outpatient visits in different practice settings." *Journal of the American Medical Association* 270(7): 835–40.

26. Gold, M., and J. Woolridge. 1995. "Surveying consumer satisfaction to access managed-care quality: Current practices." *Health Care Financing Review* 16(4): 155–73.

27. Dull, V. T., D. Lansky, and N. Davis. 1994. "Evaluating a patient-satisfaction survey for maximum benefit." *Joint Commission Journal on Quality Improvement* 20(8): 444–53.

28. Vavra, T. G. 1992. *Aftermarketing: How to Keep Customers for Life Through Relationship Marketing.* Burr Ridge: Business One Irwin.

29. Finkelstein, B. S., D. L. Harper, and G.E. Rosenthal. 1999. "Patient assessments of hospital maternity care: A useful tool for consumers?" *Health Services Research*, 34(2): 623–640.

30. Scanlon, D. P., and T. J. Hendrix. 1998. "Health plan accreditation: NCQA, JCAHO, or both?" *Managed-Care Quarterly* 6(4): 52–61.

31. Fogarty, L. A., B. A. Curbow, J. R. Wingard, K. McDonnell, and M. R. Somerfield. 1999. "Can 40 seconds of compassion reduce patient anxiety?" *Journal of Clinical Oncology* 17(1): 371–79.

32. Carey, R. G., and J. Seibert. 1993. "A patient survey system to measure quality improvement: Questionnaire reliability and validity." *Medical Care* 31(9): 834–45.

33. Koshy, K. T. 1989. "I only have ears for you." *Nursing Times* 85: 26–29.

34. Harkey, J., and R. Vraciu. 1992. "Quality of health care and financial performance: Is there a link?" *Health Care Management Review* 17(4): 55–63.

35. Williams, S. J., and P. R. Torrens. 1999. *Introduction to Health Services.* Albany, N.Y.: Delmar.

36. Merry, M. D. 1993. "Total quality management for physicians: Translating the new paradigm." Pp. 51–59 in *The Textbook of Total Quality in Health Care,* ed. A. F. Al-Assaf and J. A. Schmele. Delray Beach, CA.: St. Lucie Press.

37. Finkelstein, B. S., D. L. Harper, and G. E. Rosanthal. 1999. "Patient assessments of hospital maternity care: A useful tool for consumers?". *Health Services Research* 34(2): 623–640.

38. Mayer, T. A., R. J. Cates, M. J. Mastorovich, and D. L. Royalty. 1998. "Emergency department patient satisfaction: Customer service training improves patient satisfaction and ratings of physician and nurse skill." *Journal of Health Care Management* 43(5): 427–40.

39. Penland, T. 1997. "A model to create 'organizational readiness' for the successful implementation of quality management systems." *International Journal of Quality in Health Care* 9(1): 69–72.

40. Walton, M. 1986. *The Deming Management Method*. New York: Putnam.

41. Johnson, J. 1990. "Investors link quality of care to the bottom line." *Hospitals* (September 5): 86.

42. John, J. 1991. "Improving quality through patient-provider communication." *Journal of Health Care Marketing* 11(4): 51–60.

43. Kotler, P., and R. N. Clarke. 1987. *Marketing for Health-Care Organizations*. Englewood Cliffs, N.J.: Prentice Hall.

44. Drachman, D. 1999. "Inferring patient loyalty from patient-satisfaction data." *Quirk's Marketing Research Review* (June).

45. Sloan, M. D., and J. B. Torpey. 1995. *Success Stories on Lowering Health-Care Costs by Improving Health-Care Quality*. Milwaukee: ASQC Quality Press.

46. Ishikawa, K. 1986. *Guide to Quality Control. Second edition*. Ann Arbor: UNIPUB.

47. Womack, J. P., D. T. Jones, and D. Roos. 1991. *The Machine That Changed the World: The Story of Lean Production*. New York: Harper.

48. Veney, J. E. and A. D. Kaluzny. 1998. *Evaluation and Decision Making for Health Services*. Chicago: Health Administration Press.

49. Whetsell, G. 1999. "The history and evolution of hospital payment systems: How did we get here?" *Nursing Administration*, 23(4):1–15, 1999.

50. Besterfield, D. H. 1979. *Quality Control*. Englewood Cliffs, N. J.: Prentice Hall.

51. Montgomery, D.C. 1985. *Introduction to Statistical Process Control*. New York: John Wiley.

52. Kelly, D. L. 1999. *How to Use Control Charts for Health Care*. Milwaukee: ASQ Quality Press.

53. Taguchi, G., E. A. Elsayed, and T. Hsiang. 1989. *Quality Engineering in Production Systems*. New York: McGraw-Hill.

54. Batalden, P. B. 1993. "Organizationwide quality improvement in health care." pp. 60–74 in *The Textbook of Total Quality Management in Health Care*, ed. A. F. Al-Assaf and J.A. Schmele. Delray Beach, N.Y.: St. Lucie Press.

55. Tindill, B. S., and D. W. Stewart. 1993. "Integration of total quality and quality assurance." pp. 209–20 in *The Textbook of Total Quality Management in Health Care,* ed. A. F. Al-Assaf and J. A Schmele. Delray Beach, N.Y.: St. Lucie Press.

56. Nelson, E. C., C. O. Larson, R. D. Hays, S. A. Nelson, D. Ward, and P. B. Batalden. 1992. "The physician and employee judgment system: Reliability and validity of a hospital quality measurement tool." *Quality Review Bulletin* 18(9): 284–92.

Index